SO-AGQ-264

PENGUIN BOOKS

THE EXTRAORDINARY VOYAGE OF PYTHEAS THE GREEK

Barry Cunliffe is Professor of European Archaeology at the University of Oxford.

THE EXTRAORDINARY VOYAGE OF PYTHEAS THE GREEK

BARRY CUNLIFFE

PENGUIN BOOKS

PENGUIN BOOKS

Published by the Penguin Group
Penguin Books Ltd, 80 Strand, London WC2R ORL, England
Penguin Putnam Inc., 375 Hudson Street, New York, New York 10014, USA
Penguin Books Australia Ltd, 250 Camberwell Road, Camberwell, Victoria 3124, Australia
Penguin Books Canada Ltd, 10 Alcorn Avenue, Toronto, Ontario, Canada M4V 3B2
Penguin Books India (P) Ltd, 11, Community Centre, Panchsheel Park, New Delhi – 110 017, India
Penguin Books (NZ) Ltd, Cnr Rosedale and Airborne Roads, Albany, Auckland, New Zealand
Penguin Books (South Africa) (Pty) Ltd, 24 Sturdee Avenue, Rosebank 2196, South Africa

Penguin Books Ltd, Registered Offices: 80 Strand, London WC2R ORL, England

www.penguin.com

First published by Allen Lane The Penguin Press 2001
Published with a postscript in Penguin Books 2002
7

Copyright © Barry Cunliffe, 2001, 2002
All rights reserved

The moral right of the author has been asserted

Maps drawn by Robin Chevalier
Printed in England by Clays Ltd, St Ives plc

Except in the United States of America, this book is sold subject
to the condition that it shall not, by way of trade or otherwise, be lent,
re-sold, hired out, or otherwise circulated without the publisher's
prior consent in any form of binding or cover other than that in
which it is published and without a similar condition including this
condition being imposed on the subsequent purchaser

Contents

Preface

This story is about a Greek called Pytheas and a remarkable journey he made 2,300 years ago around the Atlantic fringes of Europe to the far north where the dense sea mists and the freezing Ocean seemed to merge. Some of his contemporaries regarded him as a brilliant scientist, others as an outright liar. Scholars who have more recently examined the evidence compare him to Captain Cook, Columbus, Galileo and Darwin. No one now doubts the truth of his claims to have journeyed to the very limits of the inhabited world – to Ultima Thule – but how he travelled, where exactly he went and what he saw are issues still as shrouded in mystery today as was the frightening north Atlantic shore in the minds of his fellow Greeks.

Pytheas of Massalia (Marseille) is our hero and his journey forms our main theme but this is also a book about 'how do we know' – of sifting the fragments of evidence, the few scraps of classical texts that survive and the contribution of many thousands of archaeological excavations, in an attempt to recreate the physical and intellectual world in which Pytheas lived and the barbarian territories he confronted on his travels. All this detective work is necessary because the book – *On the Ocean* – that Pytheas wrote on his return to the safety of the familiar Mediterranean has been lost for nearly two thousand years.

When it was first published, about 320 BC, *On the Ocean* must have been a shocking book. The Greeks knew virtually nothing of what lay 'beyond the Pillars of Hercules' (the Straits of Gibraltar). They were aware, of course, that Europe faced the Ocean, an embracing Ocean that many believed encircled the known world. They also knew that from somewhere along this mysterious interface came tin, amber and gold but that was about all. Beyond the natural barriers that contained the Mediterranean world – the Balkan Mountains, the Alps, the Cévennes and the Iberian Mesetas – lay barbarians, people so backward and destitute of culture that they could not even speak Greek but communicated in noises that resembled the braying of animals. Pytheas was the first Greek to travel among them to the limits of the inhabited world and to publish a sober description of what he saw. Many will have read his account in sheer disbelief. The world of the Atlantic fringe which Pytheas presented for his sophisticated audience simply did not conform to their comfortable preconceptions.

The scraps that survive of Pytheas' account are the earliest descriptions we have of Brittany, the British Isles and the eastern coasts of the North Sea – they represent the beginnings of north-west European history and the first glimpse the British have of their ancestors. Nearly three centuries later, in 55 BC, Julius Caesar was the next literate visitor from the Mediterranean to make a brief and faltering exploration of the more accessible parts of the island of Britain. It was to be four hundred years before anyone followed Pytheas as far north as Orkney: then a detachment of the Roman army commanded by Julius Agricola is said to have received the submission of local chieftains. Pytheas the explorer stands alone, isolated by time. He is among that small group of truly remarkable people who have, over the centuries, jolted the perceptions of their contemporaries to entirely new levels.

To research and to present the story of this mysterious scientist and his epoch-making journey and the different worlds through which he moved has been great fun. I have quite unashamedly done it by going on the journey with him, following wherever the clues have led, never quite knowing where we would end up, pausing from time to time to observe and take stock. This has inevitably led us into some intriguing byways – early navigation, Greek astronomy, tin mining, origin myths and primeval amber-producing forests. In this way I hope the reader is able to follow Pytheas and share his developing sense of wonder as the strange and awe-inspiring waters of the Atlantic opened up to him, while at the same time experiencing something of the joy and fascination of being an archaeologist.

But before the journey can begin we need to understand something of the world in which Pytheas lived – the closed world of the western Mediterranean with its coastal cities looking inwards to the sea, their backs to the hills and mountains inhabited by barbarians. It was a world of growing tension where Greeks, Etruscans, Romans and Carthaginians were competing, with increasing ferocity, for economic and political mastery.

1

PYTHEAS THE MASSALIOT

All cities are proud of their heroes. Their statues stare grandly down on us from their pedestals telling more about the age that sculpted them than about the people themselves or the times in which they lived. Marseille ancient and modern has always seen itself as a great maritime power, and on its entrepreneurial trade reputations and fortunes have been and continue to be made. Where better, then, to proclaim its ancient heroes, Pytheas and Euthymenes, than framed in temple-like niches set in the façade of the Marseille Bourse – the stock exchange – staring out across its famous enclosed harbour, the Calanque, now crammed with pleasure boats but until comparatively recently, when the size of ocean-going ships and container vessels demanded more accessible berths along the nearby coast at La Joliette, the greatest natural commercial harbour of the Mediterranean.

Pytheas and Euthymenes – shadowy figures of the fourth century BC but worthy role models for more recent city fathers. Both were adventurers prepared to move out of the comfortable, familiar waters of the Mediterranean to explore the monster-ridden Ocean beyond the Pillars of Hercules. Euthymenes sailed south along the coast of Africa, reaching at least Dakar and Senegal, and he may even have got as far as Ghana, while Pytheas sailed north, bringing back tales of tin-producing lands, islands where amber was washed up by the sea and, in the far, far north, Thule where the ocean waters congealed. 'Rubbish,' said later Greek commentators, 'the man was a charlatan and made most of it up.' Yet here he stands in a place of honour – *the* place of honour high on the front

I

of the Bourse – heavily cloaked against the northern cold, survey gear in his left hand and a beefy right arm folded across his body in a stance of aggressive protection as he stares steadfastly into the distance – out to sea. A charlatan or a heroic adventurer? A mere collector of anecdotes or an original observational scientist? These are the questions we will set out to explore.

The materials we have to deal with will lead us along many byways. On his return Pytheas wrote a book, *On the Ocean (Peri tou Okeanou)*, sometime about 320 BC. The actual Greek text no longer exists but it was quoted by at least eighteen other writers over the next nine hundred years. How many of them actually had access to an original manuscript or were quoting some secondary or tertiary source is difficult to say, but as with Chinese whispers the passing down of information has led to some curiously garbled results. How many copies of *On the Ocean* were ever made? No doubt the Massaliots had one and there must have been at least one in Athens. Copies would also have been produced for the great libraries of Pergamum and Alexandria but all have disappeared – destroyed in acts of violence or dispersed to monasteries to lie forgotten and to crumble away. The chances of a fragment surviving in one of the few remaining monastic libraries or preserved in the mud of a Mediterranean harbour waiting to be found by archaeologists are remote indeed. We must be content with what has come down to us in the works of others – and relish the challenge of making sense of it all.

But we have far more than the chance survival of a few classical texts to build our story on. The activities of archaeologists over the last century or so have revolutionized our understanding of the past. In the world of literate Mediterranean civilization archaeology has gradually built up a systematic, and largely objective, structure against which to judge the reliability of, and to create the context for, the limited array of biased anecdotes that come down to us in the guise of 'ancient history' (though I must admit that not all scholars of ancient history would be prepared to see it in this way). In the barbarian world beyond, the impact of archaeology has been even greater, creating from the earth a picture of the social and

economic development of all the pre-literate peoples. We now know
a great deal about the places Pytheas claims to have visited and the
people who lived there – far more than any of his contemporaries
could possibly have known. But even more important is that the
totality of the data now available allows us to glimpse the dynamics
of the world that Pytheas inhabited. It was a world of change,
of developing horizons, of contacts over huge distances, of
commodities and ideas flowing and knowledge expanding. The
Mediterranean states were part of a fast-growing world system
incorporating the whole of Europe and North Africa, characterized
by increasing interdependence. Tip the balance in one place, however remote, and the dislocation would be felt throughout. There
was a degree of equilibrium but it was unstable. This was the world
of Pytheas and our expanding knowledge of it enables us the better
to understand the actions of this remarkable man.

A few metres from the edge of the Vieux Port of Marseille, at the
lower end of La Canebière, a large bronze plaque has been set into
the concrete. It reads, 'Ici vers l'an 600 avant J. C. des marins Grecs
ont abordé venant de Phocée cité Grecque d'Asie Mineure. Ils
fondèrent Marseille d'où rayonna en occident la civilisation': 'Here
around 600 BC Greek sailors arrived from Phocaea, a Greek city
in Asia Minor. They founded Marseille, from where civilization
spread to the west.' As civic accounts of history go it is a straight-
forward and accurate statement although whether Marseille could
lay claim to being the sole font of civilization in the western Mediterranean might reasonably have been contested by the Phoenicians,
Carthaginians and Etruscans. A rather more questionable rendering
of the Greek arrival is to be found, somewhat inappropriately, on
the monumental stairway of Marseille's main railway station, the
Gare St-Charles. Here we are greeted by a statue of a stern Greek
matron accompanied by two healthy children riding in the prow
of a ship. The meaning of all this, made more puzzling by the
accompanying dolphins, looking distinctly like Pekinese, is clarified
by the inscription explaining the allegory – *Marseille Colonie
Grecque* – Marseille, a Greek colony.

That Marseille – or Massalia as it was known to the Greeks –

The founding of Massalia

Massalia

Alalia

Etruscans

Adriatic

Tyrrhenian
Sea

Velia

C

Ma

G

Carthaginians

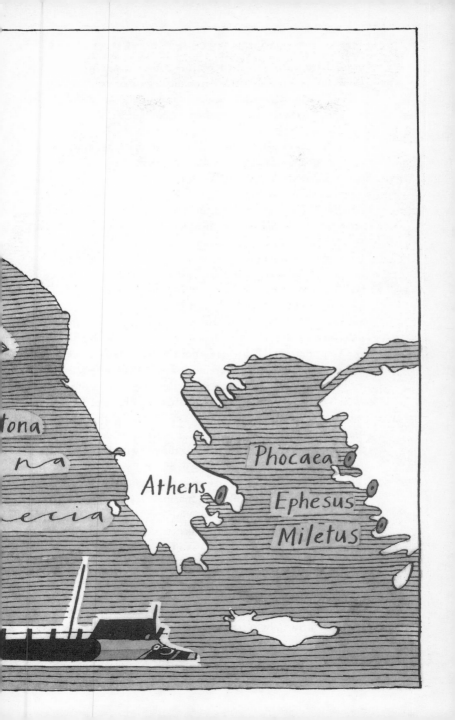

was a Greek colony is not in doubt, nor is its settlement by Phocaeans from the Greek town of Phocaea on the Aegean coast of Asia Minor (not to be confused with Phoenicians from the coast of what is now Lebanon and Syria, who colonized the coast of North Africa, parts of Sicily and Sardinia and southern Iberia). The Phocaeans were among the more entrepreneurial of the eastern Greeks, renowned, according to the historian Herodotus, for sailing in warships called penteconters to explore the Aegean and the northern part of the western Mediterranean. It was as a result of these voyages of reconnaissance that they identified potential sites for settlement, eventually choosing to establish colonies at Massalia in about 600 BC and Alalia, on the east coast of Corsica, about 565 BC.

Among the ancient writers there are two different traditions for the date of Massalia's foundation, one about 600 BC, the other fifty-five years later. The first is most likely to be correct and is given strong support by the archaeological evidence which shows that the earliest Greek pottery from the site dates to this time. How the erroneous later date came to be accepted by reputable historians like Thucydides and Pausanias is not without interest. It seems that they were simply conflating events. In about 545 the Persian armies led by Cyrus the Great, intent on establishing control of the cities of Asia Minor, attacked the mother city of Phocaea, forcing the inhabitants to flee in their ships. They made for their colony of Alalia with the intention of settling but the sudden build-up of Greeks here was seen as an escalating threat by the Etruscans facing them just across the Tyrrhenian Sea.

Until the Phocaeans had arrived in the region sixty years before, the Etruscans had controlled the maritime traffic of the northern part of the western Mediterranean and were trading widely around the shores, from the Alpes Maritimes far down the coast of Iberia. The foundation of Massalia curtailed these activities though not disastrously; but the new influx of refugees was the last straw. An inconclusive sea battle ensued, with Carthaginians weighing in on the side of the Etruscans. Although the Greeks had the upper hand, they showed considerable discretion and decided to take themselves off to southern Italy to establish a new home at Velia safe among the other Greek colonies already there. It is easy to see how the ancient historians became confused, and without the conclusive archaeological evidence for the earliest settlement at Massalia its foundation date might still be in dispute.

Leaving aside the subtleties of dates, Massalia has a splendid foundation myth. It comes in two parts: the first is recorded by the Greek geographer Strabo. He tells how when the first group of settlers were about to set out from their home city of Phocaea they received an oracle advising them to take with them a guide provided by the great temple of Artemis at Ephesus. Since no colonial expedition would dare to leave without heeding divine guidance they sailed down the coast of Asia Minor and put in at the port of Ephesus, there taking on board their guide, Aristarche, 'a woman held in very high honour', as well as a number of sacred images among which was a wooden statue of the deity, the many-breasted Artemis. The story ends appropriately when, after sailing the length of the Mediterranean, and making a successful landing at the site of their new city, they built a temple to the Ephesian Artemis to house the sacred objects and installed Aristarche as the priestess.

In his description of the city Strabo tells us that the temple of Artemis stood prominently on the headland above the harbour along with the temple of the Delphinian Apollo. Exactly where the two early temples were sited has not yet been established. Most likely they were on the high point of the promontory overlooking the harbour – now the Butte des Moulins – but it is possible that the lower hillock – the Butte St-Laurent – at the end of the promontory just above the harbour mouth was chosen. Sited here the temple would have been the first building to be seen from a ship approaching the harbour and the last to disappear from view on departure. Pytheas and his contemporaries would have found the sight comfortingly familiar.

Strabo's mention of the temple of the Delphinian Apollo is interesting. This was not the Apollo of Delphi but a different deity, a sea god, who, taking the form of a dolphin, guided ships safely across the oceans (and, incidentally, provided the iconographic reference for the pug-faced dolphins gracing the monument outside the railway station).

Another variant of the foundation myth is given by Justin, a historian of the second century AD quoting an earlier local writer of the first century BC. In this story the Greek expedition was commanded by Protis. Their arrival corresponded with a ceremony organized by the local Celtic chieftain Nannos, at which his daughter Gyptis was to choose a husband from among her many suitors. The newcomers were invited to the party and the inevitable happened – Gyptis chose Protis! Nannos accepted his daughter's choice and to show his approval gave the Greeks land on which they founded their city. It is the stuff of all good myths – love, honour and lasting friendship. What truth may lie behind it we shall never know but again archaeology allows something of the background to be sketched in.

We have said that the Etruscans were already exploring and exploiting the coastal region of what is now southern France before the foundation of Massalia. The archaeological evidence shows that already by c. 650 a lively trade had grown up – a fact amply demonstrated by the large quantities of Etruscan wine amphorae and drinking vessels found on a number of coastal sites, in particular at St-Blaise in the Rhône delta near the mouth of the river. Excavations here have shown that the site was already occupied by natives before the Etruscan imports made their appearance and with the earliest Etruscan finds there are indications of large-scale salt production and the manufacture of jewellery from coral. Taken together the evidence suggests that St-Blaise may have been the site of a regular trading port, or *emporion*, where Mediterranean luxuries were exchanged for native products. There may well have been other similar sites along the coast, places such as Cap Couronne and Tamaris, where early material has also been found.

Other finds from these early 'trading' levels include distinctive eastern Greek pottery and oil amphorae from Attica. More exotic imports, possibly from Greek workshops in the Greek cities of southern Italy, include bronze 'Rhodian' flagons for pouring wine and cauldrons decorated with griffin heads. These made their way inland into the heart of barbarian Europe, quite possibly as diplomatic gifts for the native élite. It is impossible to say whether these pre-colonial Greek goods were carried in Greek ships or were transported by Etruscans who could easily have picked up cargoes of this kind in the harbours of southern Italy – quite probably it was a combination of the two. But what it all shows is that the native communities of the coastal region were entirely familiar with traders, who for fifty years or more had been making regular summer visits to the established market sites laden with goods which the natives were pleased to acquire to display as symbols of their own prestige. It was against this background that the Phocaeans arrived about 600 BC to establish the first permanent colony: it is little wonder that the native Celts were pleased to see them. It makes the foundation myth seem almost believable.

The founding fathers will have been intent to establish two things above all, a suitable home for their gods and a constitution to rule themselves by. We have already mentioned the temples but what of the constitution? Aristotle, active at about the time that Pytheas was growing up in Massalia, was impressed by the Massaliot constitution and wrote a detailed account of it. The original text does not survive but it is referred to by Strabo three centuries later in sufficient detail to enable the main lines of government to be reconstructed. Strabo, too, was impressed: 'The government under which the Massaliotes live is aristocratic, and of all aristocracies theirs is the best ordered since they have established a Council of six hundred men who hold the honour of that office for life. These are called Timouchoi.' The word means simply the 'holder of honours' but it almost certainly connotes a wealth qualification. To be eligible for election it was necessary for the family to have held Massaliot citizenship for at least three generations and for the aspiring councillor to have produced children. The unwieldy six hundred elected an executive committee of fifteen empowered to 'carry on the immediate business of government' and a trium-

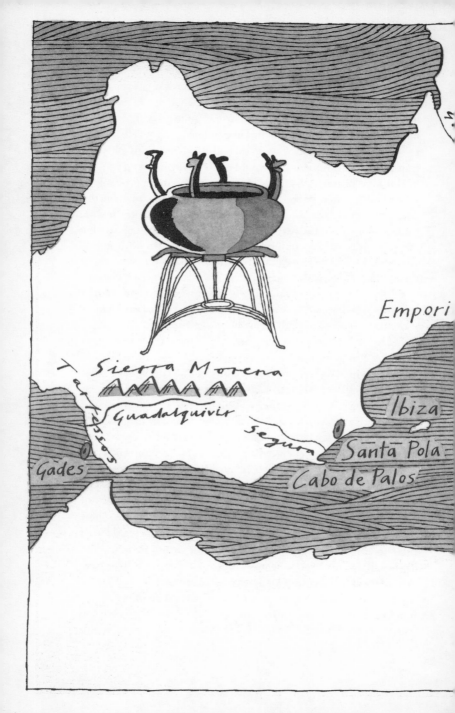

Empori

Sierra Morena

Guadalquivir

Tartessos

Segura

Ibiza

Santa Pola

Gades

Cabo de Palos

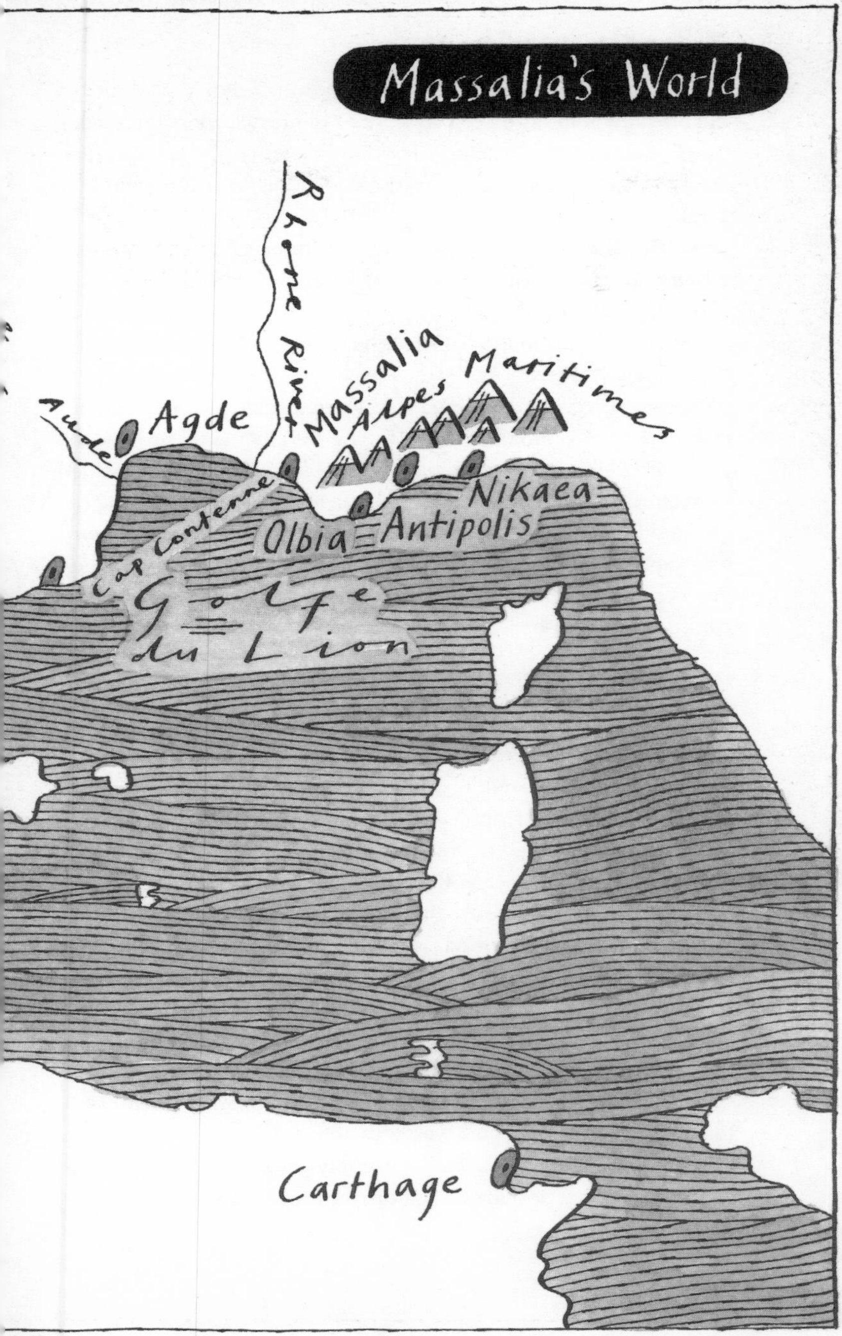

Massalia's World

Rhone River

Aude

Agde

Massalia

Alpes Maritimes

Cap Corntenne

Olbia

Antipolis

Nikaea

Golfe du Lion

Carthage

virate of these were given the ultimate power. Among the duties of the fifteen would have been to serve as military leaders if the need arose and to provide the judiciary administering the laws, which, Strabo tells us, were based on those of Ionia and were publicly displayed for all to see.

Isolated scraps of the law code, mentioned by contemporary writers, suggest a somewhat austere regime at least in theory. Women were allowed no wine, ribald theatre was forbidden and conspicuous consumption, such as heavy expenditure on elaborate funerals and expensive bridal dresses, was restricted. But there were compensations. Those wishing to commit suicide could make their case to the *timouchoi* and if convincing the city would provide the necessary dose of hemlock at no cost. Public order was maintained by requiring all foreigners to hand in their weapons on entering the city and for the dispatch of criminals it appears that a rusty sword was kept – rusty, some have suggested, not to inflict greater agony but because of under use. For the wealthy and the free it was a comfortable, well-ordered existence.

Massalia's prosperity was based on its ability to control the trade around the shores of the northern half of the western Mediterranean and from these coastal regions into the barbarian hinterlands beyond. Westwards from Massalia, across the Golfe du Lion, lay Emporion (the market), modern Ampurias. It was probably founded by the Phocaeans thirty or forty years after Massalia at about the same time as Alalia. Since it was only 'two days and one night's' sailing from Massalia it provided a convenient first stopping-point on the trade route that led down the Spanish coast towards the lucrative metal resources of southern Iberia. These were largely under the control of Phoenicians and their successors the Carthaginians, but Greeks had been penetrating the markets since the seventh century. In the middle of the fifth century a fortified Greek trading post was built at Santa Pola near the mouth of the River Segura. This was a carefully chosen location because the Segura valley provided a major route westwards to the upper reaches of the Guadalquivir valley along the north flank of which lay the silver-rich Sierra Morena, with the silver and copper resources of Tartessus further west. By controlling the estuary of the Segura the Greeks had access to the varied resources of western Iberia without having to contend with the competing, and increasingly hostile, interests of the Carthaginians, who controlled the southern coasts of Iberia and the approaching sea-ways.

Between Emporion and Massalia lay another Greek port, founded by the Massaliots, at Agde. Not only was it a convenient stopping-point on the coastal route but it was also conveniently close to the mouth of the River Aude – the first leg of an ancient and vital route which led, via the Carcassonne Gap, to the River Garonne and its wide estuary, the Gironde, a route which linked the Mediterranean to the Atlantic. We shall have far more to say of this route later, but it is sufficient now to note that it provided an axis of contact between the two oceans which had been in use for many millennia.

To the east of Massalia the narrow coastal strip between the sea and the Alpes Maritimes was lined with Greek ports, among them Olbia, Antipolis (Antibes) and Nikaia (Nice), all established by Massalia. All had fertile hinterlands producing wine and fruit and, no doubt, aromatic herbs, gathered from the upland garrigue, of the type which still enliven the flower market of Nice.

The wine production of this coastal strip from Nice to Massalia was a significant part of the Massaliot economy and is one of the activities that lends itself well to archaeological investigation. The reason for this is simple. Wine at this time was transported in thick-walled pottery containers called amphorae which, once emptied of their contents, were generally discarded. Being so robust the sherds are virtually indestructible and tend therefore to bulk large in archaeological excavations. From this unprepossessing material much valuable evidence can be gleaned. The shapes of the amphorae, changing through time, are a good indicator of date, while petrographic analysis of the amphora fabrics can usually tell in what region they were made, since heavy minerals in the clay or fine grits added as temper, once identified, may be found to be quite specific to a particular locality. Armed with these minutiae archaeologists studying amphorae from a particular site occupied over a period of time should be able to show how the quantity of imported wine varied with time and from what regions and in what quantities the wine, at any one time, was coming. In this way the subtleties of the ancient economy can begin to be teased out.

One of the tools beloved of archaeologists is the distribution map – a map showing where a particular artefact has been found. Although there are dangers in relying too heavily on these maps, not least because the evidence is always very incomplete, they can be helpful. One, of particular interest to us, shows the distribution of distinctive Massaliot wine amphorae of the type in use between 540 and 350 BC. As might be expected, they cluster in the coastal arc between Ampurias and Nice but some travelled surprisingly far, right down the coast of Italy, with a concentration around the Bay of Naples, to the southern tip of Sicily, and along the Iberian coast to beyond Cape de Palos just east of Cartagena. One interesting feature of the Spanish distribution is the number of wreck sites identified offshore – a stark reminder that not all trading enterprises were entirely successful. The map, then, shows something of the maritime reach of the Massaliot entrepreneurs but it has one or two other stories to tell. The amphorae seem to have been drawn inland along the two main river routes – the Aude and the Rhône. Beyond that a few turn up in the valley of the Garonne and rather more in the barbarian heartland of west central Europe from Burgundy across to southern Germany. Here we are witnessing quite different processes at work, which deserve some explanation.

The few amphorae in the valley of the Garonne are probably a reflection of local systems of exchange between neighbouring tribes allowing a fairly low level of exotic goods to be moved over considerable distances. Much the same pattern is reflected in the distribution of painted Greek pottery arriving in boatloads from Attica to Massalia and Agde. The amphorae and fine wares are, of course, only the archaeologically visible part of what must have

The Wine Trade

been a far more extensive 'trade'. But what passed the other way, from the barbarian world to the Mediterranean? We can only guess. Slaves perhaps – always a desirable commodity in the Mediterranean world – and it is a fair assumption that one of the most valuable of the trade goods was tin coming ultimately from southwestern Britain and Brittany. Tin was an essential component of bronze (crucial for making a whole range of things, from feasting gear and statues to brooches and hairpins), making up some 10 or 11 per cent of the alloy, but little was to be had in the classical world. The most prolific sources lay along the edges of the Atlantic, a region of which many tales were told. There can be little doubt that Pytheas would have known these stories and he may well have talked to traders about the route across Gaul via the Garonne to the Atlantic along which the metal was carried. These scraps of intelligence, as we shall see, were soon to inspire his lively curiosity.

Judging by the distribution of Massaliot amphorae, the Rhône and the Saône route was well used at this time. But it was not only wine that flowed north. Along with the amphorae went Attic cups to drink it from, bronze flagons to pour it and elaborate bronze mixing vessels like the huge krater found at Vix in Burgundy and the cauldron decorated with crouching lions from Hochdorf near Stuttgart. In fact what was finding its way northwards into the barbarian communities of west central Europe was the complete sets of wine-drinking equipment that would have graced the Greek ceremony of the *symposion* – a structured social occasion of good conversation well lubricated with alcohol. This said, it is doubtful whether the élite of western central Europe, in accepting the equipment of wine drinking, were adopting the manners and mores of the Greeks any more than the gentry of eighteenth-century England, in drinking tea poured from teapots into cups, had any serious appreciation of the subtleties of the Japanese tea ceremony. Both were simply adopting the trappings of exotic foreign behaviour to demonstrate their own social pre-eminence.

The élites of west central Europe (known to archaeologists as the Hallstatt culture after an important cemetery and salt-mining site in Austria excavated in the nineteenth century) had for centuries demonstrated their status through their command of elaborate equipment, much of which they buried with the dead. Earlier, in the seventh and early sixth centuries BC, the principal items of display included elaborate horse gear and four-wheeled vehicles which carried the dead to their graves, while lesser men were accompanied only by the trappings of their riding horses and their long slashing swords. But fashions changed, and after the middle of the sixth century a new range of Mediterranean luxury goods – principally those associated with wine drinking – became available together with greatly increased quantities of gold from western European sources and even more recherché exotics such as the oriental silk used to embroider a fabric found in a tomb at Hochmichele. It has become customary, in the archaeological jargon, to refer to this Hallstatt élite-dominated society as a 'prestige goods economy' – borrowing a term widely used in anthropology. What is understood by this is a society in which the leaders maintain their position of pre-eminence by tightly controlling the flow of exotic goods which they selectively pass down to their subordinates as gifts, providing sufficient for them to pass on some to those subservient to them. In this way a rigorous hierarchy was maintained through regularly demonstrated bonds of patronage and clientage.

Looking at this West Hallstatt society in its chronological perspective it is possible to trace the development of this system way back into the past, at least to the thirteenth century BC. In other words it was the result of local development and was not dependent to any significant extent on external stimulus. Now this raises fascinating questions. It is easy to look at the distribution of Greek consumer goods in the graves and settlements of the Hallstatt élite and to see them as the result of wily Greek entrepreneurs exploiting the simple natives of the hinterland, but social relationships are rarely that simple. Hallstatt society was selective about what it accepted from the Mediterranean world. It took only those things that it wanted and could use within its own social system rather than everything thrust upon it. There is some suggestion, for example, that the figured Attic pots were selected according to the theme depicted, a warlike one generally being preferred. In other words the relationship between Massalia and the Hallstatt élite would have been mutually beneficial. One can imagine the earliest tentative contacts, with the Greeks establishing friendly relationships through elaborate diplomatic gifts, opening the way for more regular cycles of gift exchange. Again, we must wonder what commodities the Greek world gained. Tin could have come into the system via the Loire route and there was much gold in circulation, some of which is likely to have passed into Greek hands. Other commodities, coming from the north, from the Hallstatt élite zone, probably included furs from the northern forests and amber from the Baltic coast beyond. Much amber was used in the Hallstatt burials, not least at the cemetery site of Hallstatt itself, and it was highly desirable among the Mediterranean communities. Pytheas was certainly well aware of the northern origins of amber. Like tin it came from beyond the known world – its mystery offered a challenge.

While we can be certain that large quantities of manufactured goods flowed from the Mediterranean world to the barbarians and raw materials travelled in the reverse direction, the great bulk of this 'trade' will have been what archaeologists call down-the-line exchange. An item might pass from one community to the next by some process of gift exchange and then might be passed on to the next perhaps as bride-price in friendly inter-group exchanges. A lump of amber picked up on a Jutish beach could conceivably have passed through dozens of owners by the time it reached Massalia. The trader who brought it into the town most likely had nothing whatsoever to do with procuring it in the first instance. For their part the Greek traders living on the Mediterranean coasts will have been quite content with this arrangement so long as the supplies were maintained. They would have had little desire to penetrate these murky and dangerous native systems – the barbarians of the inland region were best left to themselves.

The intensive period of exchange between Massalia and the West Hallstatt élites was short-lived. It lasted from about 540 to about 450 and was over almost a century before Pytheas was born. How and why it ended brings us face to face with the intriguing problem of the Celtic migrations.

Who the Celts were, and indeed if they ever existed as a recognizable ethnic entity, is a lively topic of debate, at least among some archaeologists. For our purposes it is sufficient to say that there is ample literary and archaeological evidence for widespread folk-movements of people, known to the Greeks and Romans as Gauls or Celts, moving southwards and eastwards from their homelands in the regions of the Marne, the Moselle and Bohemia sometime around 400 BC. Large numbers, from various different tribes, surged through the Alpine passes into northern Italy to settle the fertile lands of the Po valley. From here raiding parties and bands of mercenaries moved through the Apennines to cause massive disruption throughout Italy for more than a century. In 396 they defeated a Roman army on the Tiber and moved on to destroy much of Rome and to besiege its Capitol. The bitter memory of barbarians from the north was seared on the Roman soul. Other

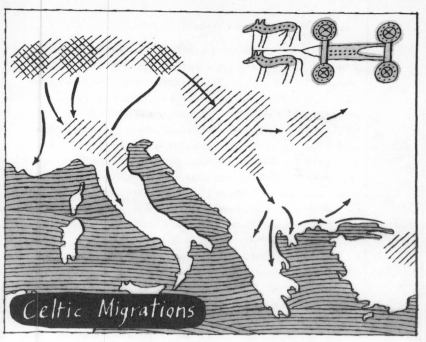

Celtic Migrations

groups moved eastwards along the Danube, settling in what are now Hungary and Serbia. From here in 278 a warrior horde thrust southwards through Greece to the great sanctuary at Delphi. They were fairly heavily mauled by the Greeks and the survivors quickly returned to join others in a major folk-movement crossing the Hellespont and Dardanelles into Asia Minor where they eventually established a state, and were still recognized – as the Galatians – in the early Christian period. From here they proceeded to raid the great cities of the Aegean coast of Asia until they were eventually brought to heel by the forces of Pergamum at the end of the third century BC. The classical world of Greece and Rome had every cause to fear the Celts.

To complete this part of the story we must consider the origins of these warlike bands. We have already talked about the West Hallstatt élite-dominated society which occupied a wide swathe of central Europe from Burgundy, through Switzerland, to southern Germany in the period 540–450 BC. Towards the end of this period new centres of élite power were developing around its northern periphery. The richest lay in the Moselle valley with another slightly less extensive in the Marne region; other centres can be recognized to the east, in Bohemia, and to the west around Bourges. In this broad arc of territory there emerged a highly innovative culture which archaeologists distinguish by the name of La Tène. It is best known for the lively abstract art style that developed, usually referred to as Celtic art. Although the new La Tène élites copied many aspects of the West Hallstatt system – aspects such as vehicle burial and the use of imported Greek and Etruscan luxury goods – there were significant differences. The vehicles used in their burials were now two-wheeled and may have been inspired by Etruscan chariots. The élite were also usually buried with a full array of battle gear including a heavy sword and clutch of spears. The growth of the new La Tène centres of power coincided with the demise of the old West Hallstatt lineages. There is even some evidence for the violent destruction of some of the Hallstatt centres. It is as though the new men around the northern fringe were taking over as the old core withered and died – rather as a mushroom ring grows ever outward.

It was in these new La Tène centres at the end of the fifth century that the 'Celtic migrations' originated. Why it was that a large sector of the population decided to move off *en masse* is difficult to say. Roman writers like Livy, looking back on these events some centuries later, were firmly of the opinion that the prime cause was over-population – there was nothing for it, they said, but for the young aristocrats to gather their followers and lead them off to new territories. There may well be an element of truth in this but in all probability the reasons were far more complex. It may be that the productive economy could no longer sustain the expectations of the élite and new systems based on warrior prestige began to take over, the raid becoming a central social mechanism. It is easy to see how escalating raiding could destabilize neighbouring regions and lead to the rapid collapse of older systems. It is a short step from this to migration, small scale at first but soon becoming an unstoppable torrent.

These are the times through which Pytheas lived. He was probably born not much more than a generation after the Celtic sack of Rome and he might even, in a ripe old age, have heard news of the Celtic devastation of Delphi. Though these particular events were distant from Massalia they were not without a significant impact.

The shadowy history of Massalia preserves two stories of these times. The first tells of the siege of the city by a local tribe of the Ligurians led by Catumandus. His name is Celtic and the Ligurians were generally regarded as Celts by classical writers. The event is not precisely dated but probably took place around, or soon after, 400 BC and is most likely therefore to have been part of the general turmoil caused by the main Celtic migrations starting in the north. Catumandus and his forces, it seems, were camped out around the city but the war leader was visited in a dream by the goddess Athena who told him in no uncertain terms what would happen to him if he did not go away. Catumandus was suitably impressed but before leading his people off, to be doubly certain he had not offended Athena, he sought the Massaliots' approval to pay homage to her at her sanctuary in the city. It is a good story, reflecting well on the honour of the city, but a rather more likely explanation of events is that some deal was struck, with the Massaliots buying off the Ligurians. This was the usual pattern of events in Aegean Asia Minor where the Celtic tribes regularly demanded, and usually got, protection money from the Greek cities. In the chronicles of Massalia the reality was probably carefully massaged in the interests of local pride.

The story is recorded by a local historian, Pompeius Trogus, who was himself of Gaulish origin, writing in the late first century BC. He goes on to note another fascinating incident. It seems that immediately after the event a delegation from the city was sent to the Temple of Apollo at Delphi to give thanks for their deliverance. Massalia had already established itself at the sanctuary by building a treasury there, probably in about 530, in recognition of the Massaliot success in the sea battle against the Etruscans and

Carthaginians off Alalia. It was natural, therefore, that they should wish to make further offerings to mark their escape from the Ligurian Celts. On returning home, so Pompeius tells us, they learned that Rome had not been so lucky and was besieged by Gauls demanding ransom (this would have been in 396 or 390 depending on which historical tradition is accepted). Since Massalia and Rome were bound in an ancient treaty of friendship the Massaliots organized a subscription for their allies, collecting gold and silver from public funds and from private individuals. This was taken to the beleaguered city to help buy off the besiegers. Needless to say the act of friendship strengthened relationships between the two cities, the Romans in return offering a new treaty which exempted the Massaliots from having to pay customs duties. Over a few generations it probably turned out to have been a good deal for Massalia – a profitable return on their investment.

So the Celts featured quite prominently in Massalia's history. They probably had an even greater, though less obvious, impact. The initial migrations of around 400 BC caused massive disruption to the economic systems which had previously bound the communities of temperate and Mediterranean Europe, and for centuries afterwards the aftershocks were still being felt. Celts were still making their way down into Italy in the third century and there was a backwash from the Celtic defeat at Delphi in 279 with some of the war bands making their way back into Europe. It was said that the Volcae Tectosages, a tribe occupying the Languedoc in the first century BC, were originally refugees from this event who had travelled the length of Europe before finding somewhere to settle. Indeed, even in the time of Julius Caesar, in 58 BC, one of the Celtic tribes of Switzerland, the Helvetii, was planning a major folk-movement to the west.

How all this was viewed by the Greek cities around the Golfe du Lion it is difficult to say but at the very least we can be reasonably sure that the old trade routes to the north had been massively disrupted. This is reflected in the attention which the Greek traders were now lavishing on the eastern coastal communities of Iberia, trying to extend their markets there. But after the initial disruption caused by the migrations of around 400 had subsided the Massaliots began to turn their attention to the north again – after all, their desire for tin, amber, gold and other commodities found in these regions was no less. This was the rapidly changing world in which Pytheas was growing up.

The city which Pytheas knew occupied a long, quite narrow promontory overlooking a large rectangular harbour then known as the Lakydon, now the Vieux Port. It was (and still is) a magnificent safe anchorage, accessible from the sea only by a narrow channel less than 100 m. wide. It was thus well protected both from foul weather and from surprise attack by sea. The promontory overlooking the harbour rises to a central spine composed of four elongated crests, St-Laurent, Les Moulins, Les Carmes and St-Charles. The first three of these lay within the ancient city, the highest being Les Moulins in the centre of the spine 42 m. above the harbour level. The promontory was given a degree of natural defence from the landward side by a marshy valley, between the hills of Les Carmes and St-Charles, which opened into a narrow projection of the main harbour. It was entirely logical, therefore, for the landward defensive wall to be built to the west of this valley to gain added protection from the marsh in front. The marsh was crossed, immediately north of the end of the harbour's 'horn', by the main road leading to the main gate of the city. Once inside, the principal street ran along the flank of the ridge, overlooking the harbour, towards the western extremity of the city – the Butte de St-Laurent – where the main temples lay, with the theatre and market place (the Agora) nearby. Below the road the port area stretched along the harbourside with its wharves, jetties and batteries of ship-sheds where in the winter months the fleet could be laid up under cover and overhauled.

It is probable that the wall totally encompassed the city though the harbour side may have been partially open. Within the protected area of 50 ha. lived the population of some 30,000 or 40,000 people. Today, impressive remains of ancient Massalia are on display in an archaeological park, created following a large-scale rescue excavation, on the site of the Bourse. The 'horn' of the harbour is clearly visible as are the magnificent city wall and gate. In the form in which we now see them they were rebuilt after Pytheas' time, but the careful archaeological work has shown that the line of the city wall and the two great square gate towers were built on foundations going back to the late sixth century BC. Standing in the park and looking towards the gate leading into the city we can fairly allow ourselves the indulgence that we are seeing – at least in topography and proportion – the approach to the city as Pytheas would have seen it in the latter part of the fourth century.

Who, then, was this Pytheas whose immediate world we have tried to sketch? If his main detractor, the historian Strabo, is to be believed, he was a poor man. By this Strabo may have meant that he was not a member of the governing aristocracy. Yet he was evidently a highly educated man and a scientist of considerable skill. Beyond this we can only guess. Was he, perhaps, the son of a well-to-do trader serving an apprenticeship as a ship's master? There is a rather ambiguous statement by Strabo that Pytheas claimed to have sailed the length of Europe from Gadir (modern Cadiz) to Tanais (on the north shore of the Black Sea). Although this has been variously interpreted, it could simply mean that he knew the Mediterranean and Black Sea well, having sailed the length of both. It is tempting to think of him moving among the seafarers and merchants on the wharves, and spending time with them in the taverns of his native city, enquiring into their varied experiences of the wider world, feeding his own curiosity until that day when finally his mind was made up. The comfortable Mediterranean world was too small and too tame; it was time for him to set out to explore the fearsome Ocean – its lands, its peoples and its resources.

2

THE WORLD BEYOND
OUR SEA

The great ports of the Mediterranean were the nerve centres of the Greek world: they were the nodes through which people passed in some number bringing with them knowledge of the world – personal observations ranging from stories they had heard of curious tribes and bizarre behaviour, to commercially valuable intelligence of the whereabouts of rare resources and precise details of the routes to be taken to acquire them. They would have brought, too, scraps of learning from older civilizations, from Babylonia and from Egypt, to feed the minds of the curious. To sit in a dockside bar (if such there were) of one of the big ports in the sixth century BC and to hear the conversation would have been a mind-blowing experience. An enthusiastic listener to all the excited chatter would have been exposed to information overload. Ever-expanding knowledge challenged convention: the comfortable myths of ancient theogony could no longer contain it all – in this way science was born.

In the more distant past the deep-seated human need to place the self in the order of things had been satisfied by creating stories about the origin of the world – myths peopled by supernatural beings – gods – who were given names and pedigrees and passions. In the early Greek world two broad traditions can be glimpsed, both eventually appearing in written form about the eighth century, one ascribed to Hesiod, the other to Homer. To Hesiod, a native of Boeotia, are credited two poems, *Works and Days* containing economic, ethical and political precepts, and an altogether different work, *Theogony*, in which were brought together ideas on the origin of the world. In the beginning was the yawning void – Chaos. Out of Chaos came 'wide-bosomed' Gaea (Earth), the mother of all things, and she produced Uranos (Sky) and together Earth and Sky gave birth to Day and Night and a clutch of other monstrous beings including Oceanus, Memory, Tethys 'and one-eyed Cyclopes, and Cronus the wily'. Gradually out of Chaos was coming form. But Cronus hated his father Ouranos and castrated him with a jagged sickle as he lay with Earth. From the blood of this act that dropped on Earth Giants, Furies and Nymphs sprang . . . and so the violence goes on with Cronus devouring his children by his wife Rhea, until he is finally outsmarted by Rhea and Zeus is born and safely raised. Eventually Zeus overthrows his father and creates the moral order of the Olympian system – the everyday gods familiar to all the Greeks – presided over by Zeus the Father of Gods and men. The *Theogony* is a remarkable, vigorous compilation which takes us from Chaos to order, from violence to harmony. The tone is didactic, with the poet using the myth to enlighten his listeners – to provide a framework against which their own behaviour might be judged. It is an explanation both of origins and of the prehistory of human emotions.

Hesiod was a mainland Greek whose world was land bound: in *Works and Days* he is disparaging about seafaring. The Homeric tradition, codified at much the same date, is that of the Ionian Greeks whose cities lined the coast of Asia Minor and looked seawards. In the creation myth of Hesiod Earth came first and gave birth to Oceanus. But in the *Iliad* the primeval entity was water – Oceanus – whose consort, Tethys, was the mother of all the gods. Here we are seeing glimpses of a separate creation myth, of a kind more readily understandable to those whose livelihood was the sea.

The myths upon which the Greeks were brought up, embedded in the poems of Hesiod and Homer and widely available in a rich oral tradition, helped the mind to come to terms with the extent and complexity of existence – they provided comfort and reassurance up to a point. But to the growing class of 'new men' – city dwellers freed from the economic necessity of producing their own food and nurtured by an increasing flow of startling information about the world – these ancient folk-tales were no longer intellectually satisfying.

It was the Ionian cities of coastal Asia Minor – all of them thriving ports – that became the hothouses of the new debate about the nature of the world. At the time when the colonists were setting out from the Ionian city of Phocaea to found Massalia, some 200 km. down the coast by sea, the great port of Miletus was thriving. Visiting the ruins today, encircled by a sombre, rather barren landscape of old marshland, it is difficult at first to see why, in the sixth century BC, Miletus became one of the greatest cities in the Mediterranean world. The answer is quite simply that the landscape has changed dramatically in the last 2,500 years. Then Miletus occupied a promontory surrounded by excellent harbours at the mouth of a great bay into which flowed the River Maeander. Around its shores other cities flourished. The bay was the terminal of one of the flourishing trade routes that extended eastwards across Asia Minor to the valleys of the Tigris and Euphrates and beyond. Miletus was the focal point where that route articulated with the Mediterranean. And so it remained for several centuries. But two natural processes combined to strangle Miletus – a subtle change in sea-level and the increased silt load brought down by the river, as the result of erosion due to overgrazing. Together they caused the bay to clog with sediment, cutting off the inner reaches to form Lake Bafa, and continued, forming a delta far out into what was once the sea. The result is that the ruins of Miletus are now surrounded by ill-drained alluvial flats with the sea just visible some 10 km. away.

By 600 BC Miletus was already an ancient port that had been in use for many centuries going back into the Mycenaean period and into Minoan times before. Later in the eighth and seventh centuries BC the Milesians were sending out shiploads of colonists to found new cities along the Hellespont, the Sea of Marmara and all around the Black Sea. Historical sources credit them with ninety new foundations which, if true, suggests that the city was acting as the agent for the disparate populations of the region, siphoning off

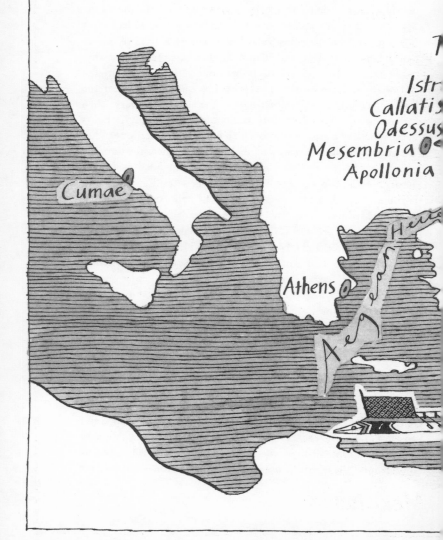

The Milesian World

Istr
Callatis
Odessus
Mesembria
Apollonia

Cumae

Athens

Hell

Ae

Olbia

Tanais

Panticapaeum

Theodosia

Phasis

B l a c k   S e a

Sinope

Heraclea   Amisus   Trapezus

gamum

iletus

Babylon

Tyre

Alexandria

the surplus – the landless young, the dispossessed, the dissipated and the adventurers – to establish the new trading centres around the periphery of the known world – all to the economic benefit of the mother city. By about 600 BC Miletus sat like a bloated spider in the centre of a vast web of trade connections – spreading north to the northern shores of the Black Sea, south to the Nile delta, overland, eastwards, to the old cradle of Babylonian civilization and westwards far into the Mediterranean. Along these strands commodities flowed and with them knowledge of all kinds gleaned from the ends of the world – ancient mathematical and astronomic wisdom from the civilizations of Babylon and Egypt and a new awareness of anthropology and geography from the more barbarous regions. The Ionian Greeks were in a unique position to begin to piece together a new world view based not on myth but on natural science.

The first of the great names to emerge was that of Thales of Miletus, born about 636 and died about 546. Thales was a person who had apparently travelled quite widely. He had been to Egypt and there had studied mathematics, quite possibly learning basic geometry, in which the Egyptians were especially proficient, including the observation that the square on the hypotenuse of a right-angled triangle was equivalent to the sum of the squares on the other two sides. This truth is attributed to Pythagoras, a native of the island of Samos, not far from Miletus, who was active in the second half of the sixth century. It is an amusing possibility that Pythagoras may have picked up the idea at Miletus from a pupil of Thales, though he could equally have learned it direct from the Egyptians.

While in Egypt Thales would also have learned something of Babylonian astronomy, sufficient to enable him to predict the total eclipse of the sun in the spring of 585. Later he put his general observation of the natural world to good use when, anticipating from his study of climate that the next season's olive crop would be unusually large, he took out an option on all the olive presses on Chios, thus owning the monopoly when his prediction proved correct. He was, evidently, a highly practical scientist.

Thales was the first of the Ionian scientist-philosophers to address himself to the question of the origin of the world, thereby implicitly rejecting traditional mythologies. He did this in a typically Greek way – by asking a simple question. What was the world made of? His answer was water. While it is possible that, in arriving at this conclusion, he was subconsciously influenced by the myth recorded in the *Iliad* that the primeval entity was Oceanus, it is the implications of the question itself that are important, since it takes with it a belief in the basic simplicity of matter and the ability of the human intellect, by reason and logic, to arrive at the correct answer. This was a major breakthrough and set the scene for what was to follow.

Thales' immediate successor at Miletus was Anaximander, some twenty-five years his junior. For him basic matter could not be a physical substance, so Thales was wrong, it was not water. Instead, he conceived of an 'undefined something', an 'Unlimited', that had no physical properties of itself but was composed of oppositions, such as wet/dry, hot/cold, all in perpetual motion. Tangible substances were made from the Unlimited and reverted to it through decay. This was a stunning intellectual leap into abstract thought and has some similarities, at a very general level, to modern atomic theory. This is not, of course, to say that Anaximander was the father of atomic physics but simply that he would probably have found it an acceptable theory quite consistent with his own general model of things.

Like Thales, Anaximander was a traveller and indeed he is credited with leading a colonial settlement from Miletus to Apollonia (now Sozopol, near Burgas in Bulgaria) on the western shore of the Black Sea. Both men developed concepts of the world. For Thales the earth was flat and floated on the surface of the Ocean. Anaximander's vision was more sophisticated. He believed in the Balance of Forces in nature. Within the vortex of eternal motion the earth hung free in the exact centre held in place by the balance of forces spinning from the periphery of the vortex. The world was like the drum of a column, a cylinder of a diameter three times its depth, with a slightly concave upper surface. He even produced a map of this surface, showing it to be governed by principles of symmetry – in effect the first map of the world. The Mediterranean was central. To the north lay Scythians, to the south, Ethiopians, with Celts to the north-west and Indians to the south-east. South of the Ethiopians was a land of uninhabitable heat, while north, beyond the Scythians, came first the land of uninhabitable cold, then the Rhipaean mountains beyond which was the land of the Hyperboreans. The entire world was surrounded by the Outer Ocean; that part to the west, joined to the Mediterranean by a channel running through the Pillars of Hercules, was called the Atlantic. This first bold concept, drawn up some twenty to thirty years after Massalia was founded, was, with a few comparatively slight modifications, to be the conceptual map carried by Pytheas at the end of the fourth century.

By the end of the sixth century Hecataeus, another son of Miletus, was beginning to make improvements to the map based partly on the results of his own travels and partly on information gleaned from sailors and merchants passing through Miletus. He was not, however, uncritical of his sources – he was quoted as saying, 'I write what appears to me to be true, for the tales the Greeks tell are many and ridiculous.' Nothing survives of Hecataeus' beliefs save as quotations in the work of others. Of these Herodotus is the most prolific and a most important original source in his own right.

Herodotus, born *c.* 484 in the Dorian city of Halicarnassus on the south-western coast of Asia Minor, is best known as the 'father of history' – the first great historian in the classical world whose works survive. He wrote on the comparatively narrow theme of the conflict between the Persians and the Greeks between 479 and 470 BC but like all good historians he provides his readers with a broad geographical and anthropological context against which to understand his epic story. His extensive travels took him to most of the major towns in Greece, all around the Black Sea and the coasts of Asia Minor and across Syria to Babylon and Susa. In Egypt he travelled down the Nile as far south as Elephantine. Such an amazing itinerary provided him with an incomparable sense of world geography. At the same time his caution as a scholar led him to reject much that was speculation. He would have grown up familiar with the old Ionian model of the world as a neatly balanced land mass surrounded by an Outer Ocean. His knowledge of a remarkable journey from the head of the Arabian Gulf clockwise around Africa to the Nile delta (about which more later) led him to accept the continuous Southern Ocean stretching from the Pillars of Hercules to the mouth of the Indus, but of the west and north he is far more reticent. 'Of the extreme tracts of Europe towards the west', he writes,

I cannot speak with any certainty; for I do not allow that there is any river, to which the barbarians give the name of Eridanus, emptying into the northern sea where, as the tale goes, amber is produced, nor do I know of any islands called Cassiterides, whence the tin comes which we use ... Though I have taken vast pains I have never been able to get an assurance from an eye-witness that there is any sea on the further side of Europe. Nevertheless, tin and amber do certainly come to us from the ends of the earth. The northern parts of Europe are very much richer in gold than any other region: but how it is procured I have no certain knowledge. The story runs, that the one-eyed Arimaspi purloin it from the griffins, but here too I am incredulous.

This is a fascinating passage. Not only does it show the cautious scientist at work setting out the limits of reasonable inference but it neatly sums up contemporary knowledge of the north – that area of mystery and rumour made the more fascinating by the tin, amber and gold that were to be got from it.

When Herodotus went to live, briefly, in Athens, his great history was evidently well under way; the year after his arrival in the city he gave a public reading which gained popular acclaim – and a not inconsiderable public reward paid in silver. Although he was willingly accepted into the intellectual life of the city, which

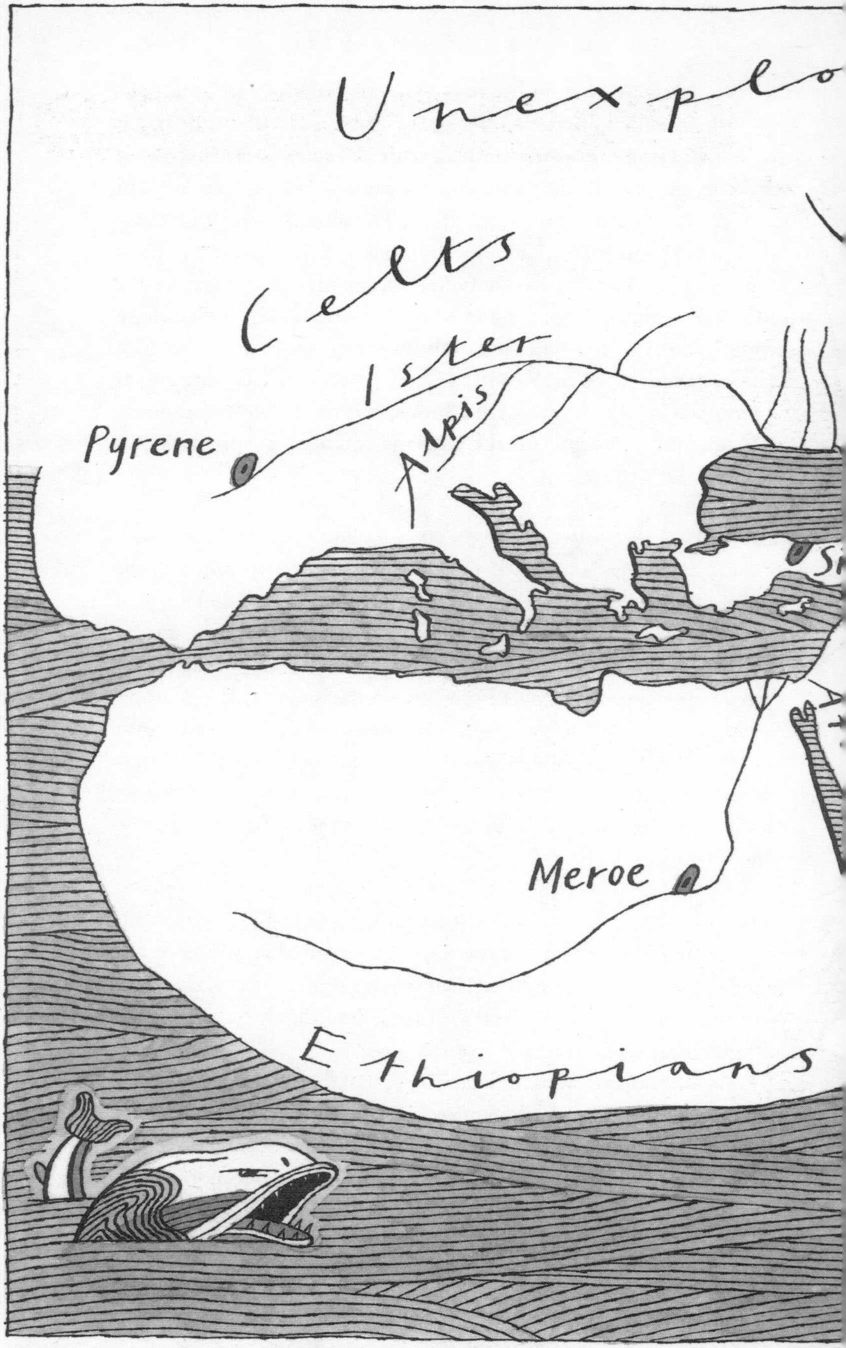
Unexplo
Celts
Ister
Alpis
Pyrene
Meroe
Ethiopians

ed

anais

Araxes

Indus

● Susa

had now begun to eclipse Ionia as the centre of creative thought, he was still an alien and as such had limited rights. It was probably for this reason that he decided to join one of the colonizing expeditions and, leaving Athens in 443, he became one of the founding fathers of the new town of Thurii in southern Italy. Here, until his death about 424, he put the finishing touches to his *Histories*.

Herodotus had probably read everything available in the Mediterranean world and had gathered a huge amount of information on his own travels. The *Histories*, then, may be regarded as a fair account of the world as it was known in the middle of the fifth century BC. Yet rigorous and all-inclusive though Herodotus was in his scholarship, he was just a little old-fashioned. His beliefs still echoed the old Ionian concept of symmetry. The courses of the two great rivers, the Danube and the Nile, mirrored each other, both starting in western mountains – the Danube in the Pyrenees and the Nile in the Atlas – flowing first east before turning inwards towards the Central Ocean. He also retained the idea that the earth's surface was a slightly concave disc. But as we shall see in a moment, science was moving on.

The *Histories* would have been widely known, not only in Greece but in the world of Magna Graecia – the heavily colonized zone of eastern Sicily and southern Italy where Herodotus was to spend his old age. By the end of the fifth century we can be tolerably sure that the educated citizens of Massalia would have known of the text and their own experiences would have broadly confirmed Herodotus' cautious view of the unknown west and north, the area from which the flood of migrant Celts was soon to burst.

Although observational science was regarded with some disdain in the intellectual centre of Athens, observations about the earth and the heavens continued to be made and some of them were very difficult to explain while it was believed that the earth was a slightly concave disc. Why, for example, did new stars appear as you travelled south and why was it that, as you went north, the polar stars rose higher and the days grew longer? All this could be explained if the earth was, in fact, a sphere. Whether or not the idea crept into the minds of those who observed and thought about these things we shall never know. What does seem clear is that the idea gained ground among the Pythagoreans in Magna Graecia, probably towards the end of the sixth century BC, more as a philosophical concept than as an explanation for awkward observations.

Pythagoras is a somewhat shadowy figure. Born on the island of Samos in the Aegean in the middle of the sixth century, he travelled widely in Egypt and the east before settling at Crotona in the fast-expanding Hellenic world in southern Italy, some time about 530 BC. There he established a brotherhood of some three hundred members, bound to each other and their master in oaths of allegiance, and dedicated to the pursuit of a regime of moral, religious and philosophical teachings. As a secret society they became deeply unpopular and were eventually attacked by a local mob who set fire to their headquarters. Some escaped though the fate of Pythagoras himself is unclear.

While the natural scientists of Ionia sought the basic matter from which everything developed, the Pythagoreans decided that number underlies everything including form: 'They thought that the whole heaven is harmony and number.' Perfect shapes were the circle and the sphere. The earth and the other heavenly bodies, including the sun and moon, must therefore be spheres and must revolve in a circle but around what? Here they hypothesized a great central fire invisible from earth because our face of the globe was always turned away from it. Ten was a perfect number. There must therefore be ten heavenly bodies revolving around the central fire. Since only nine could be identified (including the sun) there must be a tenth – which they called the 'counter-earth' – always out of sight on the other side of the central fire.

The Pythagorean model, as it is explained to us by Aristotle, was a purely intellectual concept based on a logical construct rather than observation. One wonders whether Herodotus had any knowledge of it and if so what he thought about it. He did, after all, spend his last years living in Magna Graecia where the Pythagoreans had been active. It is difficult to believe that so learned a man was unaware of such revolutionary theories.

By the end of the fifth century the concept of the earth as a globe was being explored in Athens by Socrates, or so his pupil Plato tells us, and it is clear that Socrates believed the globe to be huge in comparison with the known extent of land. Plato himself travelled extensively in Magna Graecia after Socrates' death in 399 and there would have been exposed to much Pythagorean philosophy, as reflected in his *Republic* when he writes of 'the music of the spheres'. Later he toyed with the idea of the earth being the central body around which the others rotated but finally it seems he may have reverted to the Pythagorean concept of a central fire. Plato and his followers enjoyed the intellectual beauty of the model rather than its implications for practical science: indeed to the end Plato remained dismissive of the value of observing nature, believing that such a practice could reveal only a distorted and misleading reflection of the underlying ideal – an ideal that could be visualized only through reason.

There were, however, other, more practical men at work. Such was the astronomer Eudoxus of Cnidus, one of the coastal cities of the south-west of Anatolia. His textbook on the stars, written about 370 BC, no longer survives, except in isolated references in later works, but he seems to have been the first man to attempt to measure the circumference of the earth, arriving at 400,000 stades (about 70,400 km. – to be compared with the actual figure of 40,000 km.). His method is not stated but would have involved measuring the height of a particular star on the same day of the year at two places along the same meridian as far apart as possible. This would have enabled the curvature of the earth's surface to be estimated, from which the radius and then the circumference could be calculated. Given the scope for error it is hardly surprising that his figure was significantly out – but it was a good try. He could also, apparently, determine latitude, which would have involved identifying places where the midday height of the sun, measured on the same day of the year, was the same. This is an important concept to which we shall return.

By the middle of the fourth century BC – that is during the lifetime of Pytheas – the value of observation to science was finally being widely accepted. 'We must collect facts', says Aristotle (384–322) and he did so, making many original observations of his own in the natural world and collecting together the received wisdom of the day. He readily accepted that the earth is a globe, giving, as confirmation, the observations that the shadow of the earth on the face of the moon at the time of eclipse is circular and that the stars change from south to north, but he rejected the idea of the central fire, believing instead that the earth itself is the central feature, thus, incidentally, establishing the model that was to serve unchallenged until the time of Galileo. As to the size of the earth, it must be small because of the rapid change in the pattern of the stars over comparatively short distances. In proportion, using distances provided by travellers, he estimated that the inhabited part was in the proportion of 5 : 3, E–W compared with N–S, and thought that the distance across the Ocean from Iberia to India could not have been very considerable – a view that was still held by some as late as the fourteenth century AD, giving great assurance to Columbus.

Aristotle's gathering together and rationalization of information and theories about the world was really a coming-of-age. The pieces were all in place and the size and shape of things more or less correctly established but there were still the great unknowns. The familiar world was largely restricted to the Mediterranean and Black Sea fringes and the rivers of Egypt and Mesopotamia. Beyond those favoured areas were zones of extreme cold and extreme heat and beyond that, perhaps, a continuous ocean joined to the inner sea – 'Our Sea' – by the narrow strait that flowed between the Pillars of Hercules. This is the world view that the young Pytheas would have grown up with.

The question of the Outer Ocean had intrigued people for centuries and the Straits of Gibraltar were no significant physical barrier to passage so long as one was prepared to wait for the correct combination of wind and current. Indeed as early as the beginning of the eighth century BC the Phoenicians had established a trading post on an island off the Iberian coast well on the Atlantic side of the Pillars of Hercules. They called the place Gadir. To the Romans it was Gades and to us Cadiz. From here Phoenician ships regularly sailed north up the Atlantic coast of Iberia and south down the coast of what is now Morocco but the journeys were usually limited, probably lasting not more than a few days from the home base at Gadir.

There were, however, exceptions. Herodotus records one remarkable event which took place during the reign of the Pharaoh Necho II (609–593) – at just about the time that Massalia was founded. Necho, it appears, was curious about the existence of a Southern Ocean so he ordered a flotilla of Phoenician ships to assemble at the head of the Arabian Gulf to circumnavigate Africa. Herodotus' description of this staggering expedition is commendably terse:

The Phoenicians took their departure from Egypt by way of the Erythraean Sea, and so sailed into the Southern Ocean. When autumn came they went ashore wherever they might happen to be and having sown a tract of land with corn, waited until the grain was fit to cut. Having reaped it, they again set sail; and thus it came to pass that two whole years went by, and it was not until the third year that they doubled the Pillars of Hercules and made good their voyage home. On their return they declared – I for my part do not believe them but others may – that in sailing round Libya [Africa] they had the sun on their right hand. In this way was the extent of Libya first discovered.

That last observation, which stretched Herodotus' credulity, in fact provides strong evidence of the veracity of the account because the sun would lie to the right once the travellers were south of the equator. Incredible though it seems, we must accept that these anonymous travellers made what must surely be the first circumnavigation of the African continent. The next occasion such a feat was achieved, this time from west to east, was two thousand years later. It was the journey of Necho's mariners that provided the evidence for the continuous Southern Ocean that featured on the early Ionian maps.

That the journey was planned from east to west may not have been entirely fortuitous. For at least two centuries the Phoenicians from Gadir had been exploring the west coast of Africa. Staying close to the coast, as was usual at the time, they would have had considerable difficulty forcing a passage southwards in the face of adverse winds and currents. Some progress could be made but they would quickly have realized that serious exploration southwards was not a realistic prospect. Even so we learn, again from Herodotus, of regular trade with natives, Carthaginian goods being exchanged for gold in a system which required each of the partners to lay out their wares and retreat. Only when one partner felt that the offered goods displayed were fair exchange for what they had laid out would they take them. Trade of this kind – silent trade as it is called – required the trust and honesty that would come only if both partners benefited and wanted the exchanges to continue.

There were occasional attempts to push the frontiers of exploration further south beyond the coastal Sahara. Some time, probably towards the end of the fifth century, a Carthaginian entrepreneur named Hanno seems to have made major advances into the unknown though, as is so often the case, our source of information is far from satisfactory. It appears that after his safe return Hanno set up an inscription in the temple of Baal at Carthage giving a detailed account of his travels. The inscription, which no longer survives, was copied by a Greek and after much recopying, with all the opportunity of introducing error that that entails, eventually comes down to us as a manuscript written in the tenth century AD. How much derives from the original inscription, how much is added from other stories and how much is fabrication we shall never know, but there is a certain consistency about the account and most scholars are prepared to accept it as a tolerably accurate transcription of the inscription recording an actual voyage.

The essentials of the story are easily told. The travellers set up trading bases, they were driven off by savages clad in skins, saw rivers teeming with crocodiles and hippopotamuses, watched lava from a great volcano stream into the sea and hunted creatures 'with shaggy bodies, whom our interpreters called Gorillas'. Having caught and skinned three they decided it was time to return home. How far down the African coast they had penetrated it is difficult to be sure. On a conservative estimate they must have reached Sierra Leone but it is quite conceivable that they may have got as far as Cameroun.

Another Carthaginian who, at about the same time, ventured into the Atlantic was Himilco. Pliny the Elder simply tells us that he was sent to explore 'the parts beyond Europe' but a little more information is to be found embedded in a late Roman poem called *Ora Maritima*, written at the end of the fourth century by a North African official, Rufus Festus Avienus.

Before we consider what Avienus tells us of Himilco's travels it is necessary to look at the poem itself in more detail. *Ora Maritima* is a ponderous and sometimes repetitive account of the sea coast, starting at some point on the Atlantic seaboard and ending at Massalia. It is generally believed to have been based on an ancient 'periplus' – that is, an account used by sailors as a guide to coastal landmarks. If so, the document was probably written by a Massaliot mariner since it ends at his home port, which he accurately describes. But to create his over-plush fabric Avienus patched on to this basic framework other scraps of information which took his fancy, snipped out of a variety of archaic sources. To impress the reader with his erudition and deep knowledge of the obscure classics the poet lists, in a rambling prologue, the eleven ancient writers whose work he claims to have used. The result is a jumbled scissors-and-paste compilation obscure in its geography and very mediocre in its poetry. The inelegance of the work should not, however, detract from its fascination: it is a unique collection of ancient sea lore.

There is much amusement to be had in trying to pull the text apart into its constituent elements, so as to reconstruct the separate pieces of original source material that Avienus used. Given that he seems to have been quite careless and to have imposed his own overblown style on the composition in an attempt to give it some cohesion, the task is difficult and is made the more so by the fact that his original manuscript was no doubt copied many times, introducing untold errors, before the final version, in 714 lines, was published in Venice in 1488.

One source that can fairly simply be separated out is a text of unknown authorship which describes the journey of Himilco into the Atlantic. It occurs in three separate places, lines 117–29, 380–89 and 406–15. The sample will give some flavour of the whole:

Himilco of Carthage reported that he had investigated the matter [the nature of the Atlantic] on a voyage, and he asserts that it can scarcely be crossed in four months. No breezes propel a craft, the sluggish liquid of the lazy sea is so at a standstill. He also adds this: a lot of seaweed floats in the water and often after the manner of a thicket holds the prow back. He says that here nonetheless the depth of the water does not extend much and the bottom is barely covered over with a little water. They always meet here and there monsters of the deep, and beasts swim amid the slow and sluggishly crawling ships.   (lines 117–29)

To the west of these Pillars, Himilco reports that the swell is boundless, the sea extends widely, the salt water stretches forth. No one has approached these waters, no one has brought his keel into that sea because there are no propelling breezes at sea and no breath of heaven's air aids the ship. Hence because a mist cloaks the air with a kind of garment, a cloud always holds the swell and persists throughout a rather humid day.   (lines 380–89)

But often the salt water extends so shallowly that it scarcely covers the underlying sands. Thick seaweed often tops the sea and the tide is hindered by marshy wrack. Many a beast swims through all the sea and great fear of monsters stalks the deep. Himilco the Carthaginian reported that he had once seen and tested these things on the Ocean. These things [were] published long ago in the secret annals of the Carthaginians.   (lines 406–15)

I have quoted the texts in full to give some idea of the way that Avienus uses his sources, yet below all the verbosity it is possible to sense the substance of Himilco's report – a four-month journey, shoals, monsters, mists, floating masses of seaweed and long days without a breath of wind. Taken at its face value it sounds as though Himilco sailed far westwards. This would make sense of Pliny's phrase 'to explore the parts beyond Europe'. All he found was an empty ocean bereft of anything but danger. Did he really spend four months trying to cross the Atlantic? Is he describing the Sargasso Sea with its tangle of weed and the Doldrums beyond the trade winds where a ship can become becalmed for weeks? It is certainly tempting to believe so – then what an astonishing adventure. Was it an attempt, perhaps, to discover the mythical Hesperides – the 'islands of the blest by deep eddying Ocean' – about which Hesiod wrote? We shall never know but our tantalizingly inadequate texts encourage the speculation.

The principal document which Avienus seems to have used, the periplus, was also a remarkable compilation. It was, as has been said, a guide to mariners and probably dates back to the sixth century BC, to a time soon after the foundation of Massalia when the Greeks were attempting to establish trading contacts in southern Iberia and in particular with the metal-rich Tartessans living around the estuary of the Guadalquivir. A few extracts will suffice to give a sense of its quality:

From here the promontory of Ophiussa rears up into the air. And the trip from the ridge of Arvium to this locale is two days. But the bay which spreads widely from there is not at all easily navigable by one wind. For you arrive in the middle of the bay with the west wind carrying you, the rest requires a south wind.   (lines 172–7)

Then the Cempsican ridge rises up . . . But the island called by its inhabitants Achale lies beneath it ... They say on the confines of that island the appearance of the water is never like the rest of the swell ... There the ancients recount that the sea is always churned up with dirty mud and the muddy waters are thick with filth.   (lines 182–94)

Then there is the height of the citadel called Zephyris. The lofty heights of the peak rear up from the ridge. A great elevation rises up in the air, and as if broody, a fog always hides the peak in clouds.   (lines 226–30)

Not great poetry, certainly, but to a sailor feeling his way along a foreign shore just the sort of detail he needs: sailing times, winds and recognizable landmarks. A document of this kind, brought up to date on each voyage, would have been a treasured possession passed down from one ship's master to another over the generations. It has a timeless quality. Similar sailing instructions, called *portolani*, were being used along the Atlantic sea-ways until charts began to be drawn in the fourteenth century.

But what is the date of this Massaliot periplus? There are a few clues. In describing the south coast of Iberia eastwards from the Pillars of Hercules the periplus several times mentions deserted lands 'but on this shore frequent cities formerly stood and many Phoenicians held these lands of old. The deserted earth now extends inhospitable sands ... also a city Hemeroscopium was formerly inhabited here. Now the area, devoid of dwellers, is marshy with sluggish swamp.' The archaeological evidence adds confirmation, demonstrating that many of the small Phoenician towns of this coastal region declined and were abandoned in the second half of the sixth century. A traveller in the decades around 500 BC would have been impressed by this. It seems likely, then, that the periplus, in the form in which it survived for Avienus to use, dates to somewhere around this time before the growing power of Carthage began to make these waters hostile to the Greeks.

The question which has fascinated generations of scholars is what was the northernmost point recorded in the periplus which Avienus used. The Oxford archaeologist Christopher Hawkes was, I think, right when he argued that the ultimate destination referred to was Cape Finisterra in Galicia at the north-west corner of Iberia. In Avienus' words:

Here rises the head of a projecting ridge, which a more ancient age called Oestrymnis, and the lofty mass of rocky height completely faces the warm south wind. Under the head of this promontory, the Oestrymnic Bay lies open for the natives. In it the islands called Oestrymnides stretch themselves out. They lie widely apart and are rich in tin and lead.

He goes on to say that the people are tough and proud. They work hard and are constantly involved in trade and they use boats made of hides sewn together. This section is lines 94–107. A little later there is a rather obscure passage in which Avienus appears to be talking of Iberia (Ophiussa) when he says, 'This place was first called Oestrymnis and the people inhabiting the area and the fields Oestrymnici. Afterwards numerous serpents put the inhabitants to flight and gave the evacuated land their name' (lines 154–7). The clear implication of these two passages is that an early name for Iberia, or at least one coastal region of it, was Oestrymnis.

Cape Finisterra fits well with the general description. It is a high and massively dominant projecting headland protecting the wide bay of Corcubión, which lies on its southern side, and the ria coastline of Galicia with its deep sheltered inlets and many islands. More to the point it is an area rich in tin – the most prolific tin-producing region of western Europe.

From here the periplus begins to list landmarks with some precision and to give sailing times which can, with a little imagination, be collated with the present coastline. Thus the 'Aryium promontory' five days' sailing from the Pillars could be Cape Mondego (allowing a sailing time of 100 nautical miles per day). The 'Ocean Island' could be one of the Ilha Berlenga, to be followed by the 'Promontory of Ophiussa', which best fits Cape Roca close to the mouth of the Tagus – and so the periplus continues, leading the sailor back through more familiar waters to the safety of Massalia.

If this interpretation is correct the Massaliot periplus could be seen to be the guide that led Greek sailors from Massalia to the north-west of Iberia to trade for the ever-coveted Galician tin some time around 500 BC. Who first made the journey we do not know but a comment by Pliny in his *Natural History* is worth recalling. He says quite simply: 'Midacritus was the first to import tin from the Tin Island.' Is he perhaps answering our question in this brief aside? While it is possible to see this Midacritus as a ship's master opening the trail between his home port and their source of tin, which he may well have first heard about in the ports of

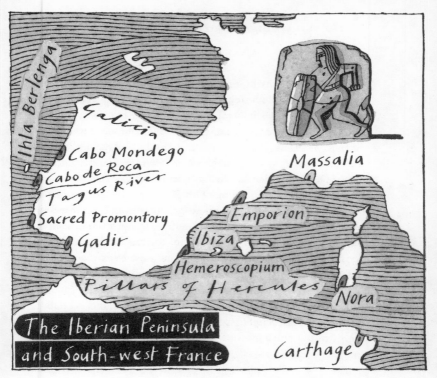

The Iberian Peninsula and South-west France

Tartessos, it is equally possible that he was an entrepreneur using a trading centre like Gadir to make up a homeward cargo composed of goods brought in by others. At any event the story of his exploits was sufficiently well known to come to the attention of Pliny half a millennium later.

One other shadowy figure deserves mention here: Euthymenes, another son of Massalia. The Atlantic, he said, is fresh water and has creatures like the Nile and it is from the Atlantic that the Nile begins, the river floods being caused by the Atlantic gales forcing sea water downstream. Perhaps he had travelled down the coast of Africa and had actually seen one of the west African rivers, or perhaps he had simply picked up garbled rumours from the comfort of Gadir. In any event his meagre fare was sufficient to win him a place of honour at the Bourse in Marseille alongside his later fellow citizen Pytheas.

Our deconstruction of *Ora Maritima* is not completely done. After first introducing the headland of Oestrymnis the poet goes on to tell us that it was two days' journey by sea to the Holy Isle, inhabited by the Hierni, and nearby was the island of Albion. This is usually taken to be a reference to Ireland and Britain, and the next passage adds details of the lands of the far north. There are clearly difficulties here if Oestrymnis is identified as north-west Galicia. Many commentators have concluded that Oestrymnis must therefore be Brittany and have supported their view by pointing out that the western part of Brittany, as we shall hear later, was given a broadly similar name by Pytheas. This, however, makes the earlier part of the periplus very difficult to interpret. The most elegant solution to this apparent conflict is to suppose that both of these dominant Atlantic-thrusting promontories were known by similar sounding names and Avienus, in stitching a quite separate tradition on to the original periplus, simply assumed them to be the same. (I have some sympathy for him. It was only after many years of hearing the BBC's shipping forecast that I realized that the frequently mentioned 'Finistere' was the region of Cape Finisterra in Galicia and not the Département of Finistère in Brittany.)

If this explanation is correct then the fragment of text which tells of the two-day journey from Brittany to Ireland and Britain, and of the northern regions, comes from a quite separate source. It could even come from Pytheas – but of this more later.

Today, with only mutilated scraps of text, scrambled almost out of recognition by many retellings and copyings, it is difficult to piece together the kind of world picture that would have been in Pytheas' mind towards the end of the fourth century. He would have known his Herodotus, by then a hundred years old, with its talk of Tin Islands and amber somewhere on the northern ocean fringe. He may well have heard stories of the voyages of exploration along the west African coast and out into the empty Atlantic, and it is even possible that he had talked to some old residents of Massalia who had heard the aged Euthymenes boast of his Atlantic exploits. He may, too, have had access to the invaluable periplus, firing his imagination for the wild Atlantic coasts of Iberia. In his early years he may even have sailed the route himself, at least as far as Gadir. But the days of free enterprise, when movement by sea was unhindered, were coming to a close as large areas of the western Mediterranean became the preserve of the hostile Carthaginians.

3

ESCAPE FROM THE
MEDITERRANEAN

When the writer of the Massaliot periplus visited Gadir sometime around 500 BC he was not impressed. In ancient times, he tells us, it was the centre of a thriving state; 'now it is poor, now it is small, now it is abandoned, now a heap of ruins.' The description caught the city at its most depressed, during the period of economic decline that swept the region at the end of the sixth century. It was a between-time. The lucrative trading enterprises set up between Phoenician colonists and the local Tartessan élite were collapsing, partly because of major political upheavals in the Phoenician homeland on the coast of Lebanon and Syria and partly perhaps because of the over-exploitation of the Tartessan metal resources. Meanwhile the successor state, led by Carthage, a city conveniently sited on what is now the Bay of Tunis, had yet to establish firm control on the west.

That the city of Gadir would rise again was not in doubt. It occupied a magnificent site – an Atlantic island just off the mainland of Iberia dominating the sea lanes linking the Mediterranean to the Atlantic. Gadir was the port from which to set out northwards to the tin-rich land of Galicia and beyond and southwards along the Moroccan coast to trade for gold and ivory with the Africans. It was also the obvious focus for more locally based trading enterprises using the rivers Guadalete, Guadalquivir and Odiel to gain access to the rich resources of southern Iberia.

Gadir – Cadiz as it is now – is one of Europe's oldest cities: it has always been a great maritime base. The old city, today tightly packed on a constricted rock platform, with its dense mass of tall buildings separated only by a grid of narrow, deeply shaded streets, looks outwards to the sea on all sides. In pace, noise and smell it belongs to both Europe and Africa. Cadiz has had a long attraction for the British since Sir Francis Drake first entered the harbour in 1587 and burned all the ships he could reach. Ten years later Lord Essex destroyed another fifty ships and sacked the town for good measure. Subsequent British attacks in 1626, 1656 and 1702 were less successful but a year-long blockade (February 1797–April 1798) and a devastating bombardment by Nelson in 1800 were to play their part in Britain's bid for naval supremacy, an action which culminated in the Battle of Trafalgar not long after in 1805. Britain's aggressive acts were not entirely gratuitous vandalism; they were a reflection of the vital strategic importance of Cadiz as a maritime base controlling the passage from the Mediterranean to the Atlantic. What was true in the struggles of the imperialist states in the early modern period was equally true in the eighth century BC when the Mediterranean trading polities were beginning to stake out their spheres of activity.

Gadir, the ancient historians claimed, was founded about 1100 BC by a group of Phoenicians from Tyre. The archaeological evidence, however, does not bear this out. Not that there has been much systematic excavation in the ancient city: the modern buildings are too close-packed and the relevant archaeological levels, where they survive, are far too deep, but at several sites on the mainland where excavations have been extensive, from Huelva in the estuary of the Odiel to the settlement of Torre de Doña Blanca just opposite Gadir, there is no real trace of Phoenician influence before about 770–760 BC. For this reason many archaeologists argue for a foundation date for the colony of Gadir of about 800 BC. But some, mindful that absence of evidence is not evidence of absence, prefer to leave the matter open, pointing out that there is increasing evidence of maritime contact between east and west Mediterranean from as early as the thirteenth century BC and that it would not be at all surprising if limited expeditions from the fast-developing Phoenician city of Tyre had sailed beyond the Pillars of Hercules to explore the possibilities for exploitation. These entrepreneurs would soon have learned of the rich metal resources of Tartessus and of the Atlantic façade beyond but the distances were too great and the demand too undeveloped to make such arduous journeys worthwhile at the time.

By the end of the ninth century, however, things had changed. The Assyrian empire was at the height of its power and demanded huge quantities of raw materials to sustain itself, not least silver, which was now the main medium of exchange. The Phoenician cities of the Levant coast were admirably situated to act as middlemen and so their trading expeditions trawled increasingly wide. A colony seems to have been established at Nora in southern Sardinia in the ninth century and Carthage was founded opposite on the coast of Africa just before 800 BC. It was probably at about this time that another group of settlers took possession of the islands of Gadir.

In Phoenicia the new town was called *Gdr*, made more pronounceable as *Gadir*, but to the Graeco-Roman world it was variously known as *Gadeira, Gedeiroi* and *Gades*. The plural form was used because the city spread over three islands. The actual settlement was on the northernmost of the islands known as Erytheia (the site of the present old city of Cadiz), which at that time had two rocky projections extending from the western side with a fine protected harbour between. A rise in sea-level and silting have changed the topography but the former promontories can still be traced not far below the sea. Erytheia was separated by a narrow channel from a long narrow island, Kotinoussa, which served as the main burial ground for the city. At its southern end was a temple dedicated to the Phoenician god Melqart, who later became conflated with the Graeco-Roman Heracles–Hercules. The sanctuary of Melqart was famous throughout the Mediterranean world. Julius Caesar consulted its oracle and the later emperors Trajan and Hadrian, both Spanish by birth, gave the cult their imperial patronage. The third island, Isla de León, was also used as a cemetery. Now, as the result of sea-level changes and silting, the original islands are joined together with the mainland beneath the sprawl of the modern city.

At the opposite end of the Mediterranean the early sixth century saw major political readjustments that were to have repercussions in the central and western Mediterranean. The most far-reaching single event took place in 574 when, after holding out for thirteen years, the city of Tyre lost its independence to the Babylonians led by Nebuchadnezzar. The other Phoenician cities of the Levantine coast succumbed to the new superpower at about this time. All this may seem remote from the affairs of Massalia and Gadir, but not so. The Mediterranean was fast becoming an interdependent economic entity – throw a rock into one end and the ripples would be felt at the other.

The loss of independence of Tyre and its fellow trading cities left the Phoenician colonies in the central and western Mediterranean on their own – the umbilical cord had now been cut, freeing the offspring to fend for themselves. Out of the uncertainty Carthage soon emerged as the leader. Its situation on the lush Bay of Tunis, controlling the wide straits between the eastern and western Mediterranean, gave it a commanding position from the start. It was the natural port of call for ships sailing east to west along the North African coast and for those making for Sicily and Sardinia as well.

Almost immediately Carthage set out to assume for itself a dominant role. One of its earliest exploits, in the middle of the sixth century, was to take over control of the island of Ibiza. Ibiza was already a successful trading base which had been founded by Gadir nearly two centuries earlier. A glance at the map shows the island's crucial importance to shipping. Vessels leaving the Punic ports in south and west Sardinia sailing due west could put into the safe harbours of Ibiza before continuing on to the coast of Iberia, arriving off Cabo de la Nao after barely 60 nautical miles of sailing. Thereafter the western route led along the Iberian shore. By controlling this more northerly route, as well as the African coastal route, the Carthaginians were now laying claim to the whole of the southern half of the western Mediterranean, absorbing into their growing sphere of influence all the old Phoenician ports, including Gadir.

In striving for economic monopoly of the sea routes Carthage was not, at least at first, contesting the rights of the Etruscans and their successors the Romans to the more northerly waters: it was the maritime activity of the Greeks they were concerned to limit. We have already seen that the Carthaginians worked with the Etruscans to deflect the Phocaean Greeks from establishing themselves at Alalia in about 537. A few years later in 509 we find them establishing a treaty with Rome. Polybius records the details:

On these conditions there will be friendship between the Romans and their allies, and the Carthaginians and their allies. Neither the Romans nor their allies may sail beyond the promontory that is named the Beautiful unless they should be obliged to do so by storms or enemy pursuit. Whosoever will be forced there will make no purchase on the market nor shall he take more than is necessary for replenishing the ship or making sacrifices, and he shall leave within five days . . .

and so on. It is a fascinating document, precisely drawn up to delimit the individual spheres of commercial activity of the two powers. Respect for each other's mutual interests continued for a further two centuries with new treaties agreed in 348 and again in 306. All this time the real enemies of the Carthaginians were the Greeks. The reason is not difficult to appreciate. The island of Sicily commanded the narrow sea between the toe of Italy and the northernmost tip of the North African coast. In the period of colonization the Phoenicians had established themselves at the western end while the Greeks occupied the east overlooking the Straits of Messina to the Greek-settled coast of southern Italy beyond. Together, the Greek towns of Magna Graecia, as the region was known, formed a formidable alliance both commercial and military.

Fighting broke out between rival factions at various times in the sixth century and continued sporadically throughout the fifth. To begin with the Greeks won a resounding victory over the Carthaginians near Himera on the north coast of Sicily in 480 but by the end of the century, between 409 and 406, the Carthaginians were in the ascendancy, taking the Greek cities of Himera in the north and Selinus, Agrigentum and Gela along the south coast. After a counter-offensive by Dionysius of Syracuse an agreed frontier was drawn up between the two spheres in 397; an uneasy truce lasted for the next fifty years.

In 342 violence broke out again, the Greeks this time being led by a general, Timoleon, from Corinth. The confrontation lasted for four years until a peace was concluded. In 318 trouble began again, the Greeks now being led by a local man, Agathocles, ruler of Syracuse. At first Agathocles suffered several setbacks in Sicily, not least the siege of his own city, but he finally decided on an audacious tactic – to take the war to Carthage. This he did by landing his army at Cap Bon – the wide and highly fertile promontory facing Carthage across the Bay of Tunis. The desultory campaign which followed continued until his death in 289. But in one very telling description the Sicilian historian Diodorus describes what the Greek armies saw in the North African homeland of Carthage:

gardens and orchards of all kinds . . . no end of country houses built luxuriously and white washed, which attested the wealth of their owners . . . land cultivated partly as vineyards and partly as olive groves, and also abounds in other fruit trees . . . herds of cattle and flocks of sheep . . . and in neighbouring pastures . . . grazing horses.

His summing up says it all: 'In a word, there was much wealth in that region, because the more noble Carthaginians had their possessions there and, thanks to their resources, they could devote themselves to enjoying the pleasures of life.'

The message was loud and clear – here was a highly desirable fertile land – a land that deserved to be conquered. When, two centuries or so later, the Elder Cato made his famous gesture by throwing down fresh Carthaginian figs before the Roman Senate to the cry of 'Carthage must be destroyed' he was vividly demonstrating two truths – Carthage was very close, too close for comfort, and the territory of Carthage was exceptionally prolific. His message was not lost and in 146 BC the armies of Scipio reduced the great city to smouldering ruins and appropriated its lands.

But we have strayed too far forward in time. As far as our story is concerned the fourth century saw intermittent warfare between Greeks and Carthaginians. It was fought out over the island of Sicily but was symbolic of a wider conflict which engulfed the western Mediterranean – an economic struggle to control maritime trade. While desultory war games were being played out in Sicily, the Carthaginians were systematically strengthening their hold on the Mediterranean coast of Algeria and Morocco, legitimizing their presence on Sardinia and taking over all the old Phoenician ports of Iberia from Ibiza to Gadir. As a result the whole of the southern part of the western Mediterranean, and the approaches to the Pillars of Hercules, became a Carthaginian preserve and as such was now hostile to all Greek enterprises. This said, it is difficult to know just how the hostility manifested itself. Were Greek ships prevented from entering these waters and were the Straits of Gibraltar entirely closed to Greek vessels? This has long been assumed to have been the case but were there interludes, say between 338 and 318, during which there was deadlock in Sicily, when restrictions were relaxed and Greek ships could slink out into the Atlantic? It is at least a possibility. But in the long perspective it is certainly fair to conclude that the period of 500–250 was a time when Greek activity in the southern and western parts of the western Mediterranean was severely restricted. The sources of silver and copper in Andalusia and gold and tin in Galicia were no longer available on a regular basis to the Greek world. The merchants of Massalia had to begin to look in other directions for their supplies.

Now the scene is set and it is time to bring to centre stage the enigmatic Pytheas – sailor, merchant, scientist, explorer – however we may choose to style him. The stark reality was that in the increasingly competitive world in order to survive Massalia had to find new markets and gain monopolies over new sources of raw materials. It needed entrepreneurs prepared to risk all in exploring the unknown. This was the challenge that Pytheas decided to accept.

How he escaped from the confines of the Mediterranean is a question that has been much discussed. One view is that the 'Carthaginian blockade' was something of a myth and that there were times when Greek ships could freely pass through the Straits. A

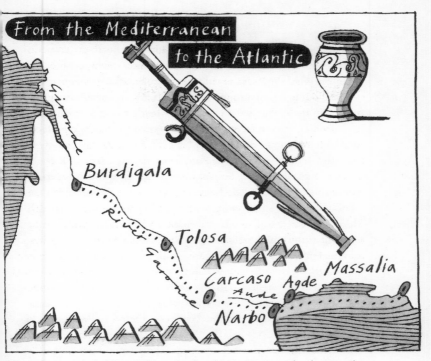

refinement of this argument is that his journey took place in the period 338–318 when hostilities in Sicily had abated. Such a dating would fit with other evidence which suggests that the journey probably took place about 325. Another interesting suggestion is that, instead of sailing all the way in his own penteconter, he used local ships, changing vessel from port to port. If this were so he might have picked up a Carthaginian trading vessel, somewhere along the south-east coast of Iberia, perhaps at the port of Hemeroscopium, which took him direct to Gadir where he could have found another vessel going north to the tin ports of Galicia, and so on. This idea has much to commend it, not least because it was travel on the cheap. To mount even a one-ship expedition would have involved considerable cost and Pytheas, we are told by Strabo, was not a rich man. None of this, of course, proves anything: all we can do is to explore the possibilities.

There is another suggestion, which I find the most convincing. If the main aim of Pytheas was to explore the northern coasts of Atlantic Europe and its tin and amber resources, why waste weeks sailing around the Iberian peninsula when he could travel overland via the Aude and Garonne to the estuary of the Gironde and take ship there? Since the route was already a major trading axis along which the northern tin came, it would have been a perfectly reasonable thing to do to travel backwards, as it were, following the route to its source. The sea trip from Massalia around Iberia to the Gironde would have been about 3,200 km., while the overland route was only about 500 km. Leaving Massalia by ship, Pytheas could have sailed due west to the Greek port at Agde and then down the coast to the estuary of the mouth of the River Aude, landing at the native port of Narbo, a total distance of about 130 nautical miles – some two days of sailing time at the most. From Narbo the overland route would first have followed the valley of the Aude as far as the hill town of Carcaso (modern Carcassonne) and then through the lowland corridor between the Montagne Noire and the foothills of the Pyrenees – the route followed now by the Canal du Midi – to Tolosa (Toulouse), the principal town of the Tolosates. From here river transport could have been used for the journey downstream to the vicinity of Burdigala (Bordeaux), the highest point which sea-going vessels could reach. At Burdigala he could have picked up one of the many ships sailing along the coastal route northwards from the Gironde to Armorica. The distance from Narbo to Burdigala was barely 400 km. more than half of which was by river. The total journey could easily have been accomplished in seven to ten days.

That the route was indeed well used at this time is shown by the distribution of Massaliot wine amphorae all along it and by the occurrence of Greek red-figured pottery at the native towns of Carcaso and Tolosa. In short, if Pytheas' primary concern was to reach the Atlantic it would have been entirely sensible for him to have chosen the well-established overland route. But did he?

One way to approach the question is to ask whether there is any hint in the corpus of observations ascribed to Pytheas to suggest that he sailed around Iberia. There are in fact two references linking him to Iberia, both quoted in the *Geography* of Strabo. The first is a sneering remark: 'These then are the statements of Pytheas, and after having returned from there [the far north-west], he traversed all the ocean-coast of Europe from Gadeira as far as Tanais' (*Geog.* 2.4.1). This statement has been variously interpreted, but taken at its face value it would seem to imply that Pytheas was simply claiming that after his northern exploration he sailed extensively in the Mediterranean and the Black Sea. The phrase 'from Gadeira [to] Tanais' was used metaphorically by other classical writers to mean the length of Europe, Gadeira and Tanais being taken to be the extreme western and eastern limits. It carries with it no more geographical precision than someone today saying 'a journey to Timbuctoo', meaning to some distant and obscure place.

The second statement (*Geog.* 3.2.11) is more intriguing. Here Strabo lists several observations about the Atlantic coast of Iberia, which he copied from Eratosthenes, warning that another writer, Artemidorus, disagrees with them. The list includes the distance from Gadeira (Cadiz) to the Sacred Promontory (Cape St Vincent), the observation that the ebb-tide finishes at this point and, finally, that the northern parts of Iberia 'offer easier passage to Keltikē than if you sail by the Ocean'. At the end of the list refuted by Artemidorus, he adds 'and in fact every other statement which he [Eratosthenes] has made in reliance upon Pytheas'. Now, while the implication of this might seem to be that all the observations originated with Pytheas, it may equally be read that Pytheas was responsible only for the last. The distance of the Sacred Cape from Gadeira and the observation on the tide is the kind of information that Eratosthenes could have acquired from a variety of sources, such as the Massaliot periplus, or from talking to sailors from Gadir familiar with the Atlantic coast of Iberia. Eratosthenes of Cyrene was head of the famous library of Alexandria from about 234 to 196 BC, where he wrote his three books, the *Geographica*, now lost apart from passing references in Strabo. At the library he would have had access to all the major texts and could have chosen freely to fill out his work.

Whatever other sources Eratosthenes used, his comment on northern Iberia was evidently based on a statement recorded by

Pytheas. What Pytheas seemed to be saying was that it was quicker to reach the northern ports of Iberia from Keltikē (that is, Gaul) than by sailing around Iberia – an entirely accurate observation, as a glance at the modern map will show. It is a fact which he could have learned from sailors he met in the Gironde and indeed he might have made a detour to see for himself. Strabo rejected the statement along with the others because it did not conform to his own cognitive geography. Yet to anyone making the cross-peninsular journey the observation would have been entirely understandable.

The two references to Iberia attributed to Pytheas, therefore, in no way require us to accept that he sailed around the peninsula, though in discussions of fragmentary ancient texts such as these there can seldom be any certainty. Yet, balancing the textual and archaeological evidence and what we can deduce of the political situation in the western Mediterranean against the simple reality of geography, it does seem marginally more likely that Pytheas chose the overland route, following the well-trodden path of generations of traders before him, rather than opting to spend unnecessary time at sea attempting to circumnavigate Iberia.

If we are correct, the route he took roughly coincided with a cultural divide between two broad ethnic groupings, the Aquitanians to the south and the Celts to the north. There are no observations on the subject attributed to Pytheas himself but the point was quite explicitly made by Julius Caesar two and a half centuries later and is borne out by some archaeological evidence. The language spoken along this route would have been what linguists have chosen to call 'Celtic' – the language known to have been common to much of Gaul at the time it was absorbed into the Roman empire in the late first century BC and which was also spoken in the British Isles. As it was the indigenous language of the hinterland of Massalia, Pytheas and his fellow Greeks would have been familiar with it, hearing it in daily use in their cities among the lower classes. Indeed, he may have been able to communicate in Celtic himself, but if so his southern dialect would probably not have been entirely intelligible to Celtic-speakers in the north any more than today the Bretons can easily understand Welsh, though the two languages are closely similar. It would not have been difficult, however, for Pytheas to find natives who knew sufficient of the various dialects of Celtic to act as interpreters throughout his journey.

Arriving at Burdigala Pytheas is likely to have looked for a native ship of the Atlantic coast to take him northwards. For this next stage of his journey we have some geographical precision, though it survives in a rather garbled form quoted by Strabo. The essence of what Pytheas seems to have recorded in his original book is the existence of a long westerly projection of the European mainland – the Greek word is *kyrtōma* literally meaning hump – of length 'not less than 3,000 stades'. At its Atlantic extremity there were various promontories, 'especially that of the Ostimioi which is called Kabaion, as well as the islands off it . . . the farthest of these, Ou[e]xisame lies three days' voyage away'. This westerly projection lay north of Iberia and was part of Keltikē (*Geog.* 1.4.5).

In recording this Strabo is careful to point out that he is simply repeating what Eratosthenes wrote and that Eratosthenes was basing himself on Pytheas. Since none of it fitted with Strabo's preconception of European geography he simply dismissed it all as 'fabrications of Pytheas'. Later, however, he backtracks a little in his criticism when he mentions that the Osismii (Pytheas calls them Ostimioi) 'live on a promontory that projects quite far out into the ocean', adding, 'but not as far as he [Pytheas] and those who have trusted him say' (*Geog.* 4.4.1).

The real geography is not in doubt. The *kyrtōma* must be the Armorican peninsula, in which case the westernmost island, Ouexisame, is most likely to be Ushant, 20 km. off the west coast of Finistère and a vital marker to anyone rounding this spectacular but dangerous coastline. Of the many promontories of Armorica, Pytheas names one, Kabaion, which most commentators take to be the most south-westerly – the Pointe du Raz, with the Îles de Sein lying out to sea to the west. The passage between the islands and the headland is eagerly sought by all sailors attempting to navigate safely around the south-western tip of Armorica. It is surely no coincidence that the two places actually named were those that would have been known to everyone sailing in these waters.

The westernmost part of the projecting land mass was occupied by the Ostimioi or Osismii and to reach Ouexisame (Ushant) took 'three days' voyage'. This would be entirely consistent with the sailing time needed for the direct route from the Gironde. Strabo's '3,000 stades' for the projection of the promontory is probably the result of his own calculation based on the rule of thumb that a day's sailing covered a thousand stades. Strabo found all this very hard to accept because it simply did not fit with his view of what Atlantic Europe looked like. To him the coast of Keltikē ran roughly straight from the Pyrenees in a north-easterly direction, separated by a channel from Britain, and from the north coast of Iberia there was open sea until Ireland was reached. While this is generally correct it did not allow for a massive peninsula – the Armorican peninsula – extending westwards. Strabo's first reaction, that it was all fabrication, gave way, as we have seen, to the more moderate view that Pytheas was exaggerating. The 3,000 stades (870 km.) which Strabo assumed to be the length of the westerly projecting land mass is indeed too long for the Armorican peninsula, which from the Loire mouth to Pointe du Raz is only about 200 km., but the error was his own in supposing that the three-day voyage from the Gironde was due west when, in fact, it was north-west, curving around the edge of the Bay of Biscay.

The implication of the text is that the journey to Ushant was made in one haul. This is not at all unreasonable and could have been done with ease by staying well offshore and keeping Île d'Oléron, Île d'Yeu and Belle-Île in sight as landmarks. Nowhere does Pytheas claim that he went ashore on the mainland of Brittany, yet it is difficult to believe that once here a man of his curiosity did not take the opportunity to disembark and later to use local vessels to explore at least some parts of the coastal region. There is, in fact, one scrap of evidence which proves that he did – the chance survival of a single scientific measurement.

Pytheas was well known throughout the ancient world as an observational scientist with a particular interest in astronomy and it is through the work of one of his admirers, Hipparchus, the greatest of the ancient astronomers, who worked on Rhodes in

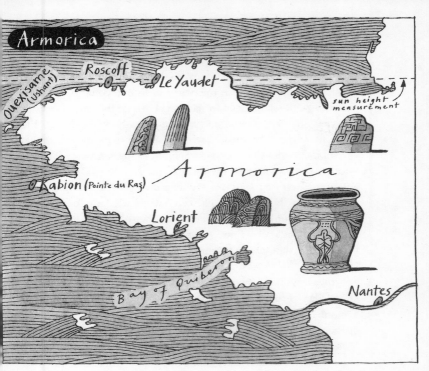

Ouexisame (Ushant)

Roscoff

Le Yaudet

sun height measurement

Armorica

Kabion (Pointe du Raz)

Lorient

Bay of Quiberon

Nantes

the late second century BC, that we learn of some of Pytheas' contributions to the study. Hipparchus wrote a *Commentary on the 'Phenomena' of Aratos and Eudoxos*, parts of which survive, and a criticism of the theories of Eratosthenes, *Against Eratosthenes*, no longer extant but referred to on several occasions by Strabo. In the *Commentary* Hipparchus discusses the night sky and the North Pole. We, of course, are used to locating true north by identifying the pole star, which we accept as immovable. Did not, after all, Shakespeare have Caesar say, 'I am as constant as the Northern Star'? But in reality the position of the stars in relation to true north varies and in the late fourth century BC locating true north was more difficult. On this Hipparchus is quite explicit: 'no single star lies at the pole, but an empty space near which lie three stars. The spot marking the pole, aided by these, encloses a figure nearly resembling a quadrilateral – exactly, in fact, as Pytheas the Massaliot says.' Here is praise indeed!

One of Hipparchus' many achievements was to calculate the latitude of a number of locations, enabling him to begin to create an accurate map insofar as the places measured could be put into a north–south relationship to each other. To do this three pieces of information were required. He had already worked out the obliquity of the sun's apparent path and a figure for the circumference of the earth. All he needed, then, was a measurement for each location to be plotted in the form of the ratio of the height of a gnomon (surveying staff) to the length of the shadow it cast at noon during the summer solstice. But since it was possible to estimate the sun's maximum height at the solstice measurements could be taken at other times and corrected so long as the interval between the date of the reading and the date of the solstice was known.

Pytheas, working two hundred years before, and without the knowledge to convert his observations to absolute latitudes, made a number of gnomon measurements, presumably to check his distance northwards from the parallel of his own home town, Massalia, the relative position of which he had already established. It was these measurements that Hipparchus utilized in his own work, and duly credited. That Pytheas actually set out to chart his journey as accurately as he was able shows a remarkable degree of well-trained intellectual curiosity. Besides his fixing of the location of Massalia, four of the other measurements he took are known. One of these related to Armorica. And since accurate measurements of this kind could be made only on land it follows that Pytheas must have gone ashore.

Where exactly he made his observation it is impossible to say, not least because of the various small errors inherent within the calculation, but the latitude works out, in modern terms, to be at about 48°42′, though a reasonable margin of error must be allowed. This parallel, so Strabo tells us, would pass 'right through the Ocean coastline of Keltikē' and so indeed it does, cutting across the Tregor – the northernmost region of Brittany – roughly through the town of Lannion and touching the coast again further west at Roscoff. Although we cannot take the calculated latitude as the *exact* line, somewhere along which Pytheas took his measurement, it is safe to assume that he made his observation at some point on the north Brittany coast between the Baie de Morlaix and the Baie de St-Brieuc. Here he would have set up his gnomon to take a precise measurement of the sun's height. Then, knowing how long it was to the summer solstice (if it was not actually the solstice), he would be able to calculate the sun's height on that day and from this to work out that he was 3,800 stades north of the parallel of his home town. What he was not able to calculate was how far west he was.

It is very tempting to try to identify where Pytheas may have landed. If he was travelling on a local boat it is likely that they put into a regularly used port. Here coincidence takes over, for the only Iron Age port at present known in the region is Le Yaudet on the estuary of the River Léguer, which lies very close to the calculated latitude. The coincidence is that since 1991 a French colleague and I have been conducting a research excavation here, quite oblivious of Pytheas' first calculated distance measurement. However, in spite of the evident importance of Le Yaudet in the Iron Age, it would be quite wrong to over-sell the site as Pytheas' landing place. It does, however, deserve some mention as a port and settlement in use at about the time of his journey.

Le Yaudet is a startlingly beautiful site – a promontory of granite commanding an estuary at the point where the River Léguer reaches the sea. To the south-west a long narrow inlet provides a perfect, sheltered anchorage with easy access to the open sea, while on the other side of the promontory a bend in the river provides deep water close against the land. We chose Le Yaudet as the site of a long-term excavation because of its ideal location as a maritime trading base and knowing that Iron Age and Roman material had been found there. What we have so far been able to show is that the promontory was in continuous use from the Late Bronze Age, about 900–800 BC. It was probably first defended at this time and was redefended on a more substantial scale some time about 100 BC and on two subsequent occasions before Caesar conquered the area in 56 BC. The size of the site and the massive nature of the defences is a fair reflection of its local importance – an importance most likely based on its inhabitants' command of the sea and of maritime trade. Some indication of this comes from the pottery found during the excavation. Among the many thousands of sherds so far recovered were a few of distinctive vessels made in south-west Britain, probably in Devon. The sherds in themselves are not particularly impressive but they do demonstrate direct cross-Channel contact between Armorica and south-western Britain in the second and first centuries BC. Pots of this kind are unlikely to have been items of trade in their own right but were probably containers for something more in demand – some delicacy perhaps taken on board as one of the many commodities making up the cargoes carried between the two Atlantic peninsulas.

Since Le Yaudet was a functioning port at the time that Pytheas was visiting the Tregor it is conceivable that the local vessel that carried him along the northern coast of Armorica, from Ushant or thereabouts, put in to one of Le Yaudet's harbours. It is even possible that he made his measurements from the headland itself and here later negotiated a passage on a boat planning to make the cross-Channel trip to Britain. The entire scenario is, of course, purely speculative and serious archaeologists should not allow themselves such flights of fancy . . . yet standing on the heights of Le Yaudet on a brilliant summer afternoon and watching the small ships come and go it is difficult not to look down to the long narrow bay below and wonder . . .

How long Pytheas stayed in Armorica is unknown. His visit could have been fleeting but equally he could have chosen to stay a while and explore this alien land. He would have found a countryside densely populated around the coasts and estuaries but rather more empty in the interior as the farmland gave way to dense forests and upland moorland. Until recently little was known of Iron Age settlement in Brittany but in the last few years aerial photography has shown that beneath the present agricultural landscape lies a much earlier one packed with small oval-shaped and rectangular enclosures with cultivation plots around them. Where survey has been systematic, as it has in parts of the Morbihan, the settlements are barely a kilometre apart. It is, of course, impossible to say without excavation that all were of Iron Age date and that all were in use at the same time. The excavations that have taken place, however, point to the Iron Age as being a time of population expansion. They also show that, once established, settlements were long-lived.

Most of the enclosures would have been the homesteads of families or extended families, comprising a few houses and a granary or two, a rick stand, a byre and the muck heap so essential for providing manure to fertilize the fields. The harsh acid soils of parts of the peninsula were hungry and needed much nurturing to produce good crops. Near the coast seaweed was often hauled up and used as well as loads of sea shells spread to counteract the acidity of the soil. All this can be seen from the potsherds from the domestic midden, rounded pebbles once attached to the roots of seaweed and the fragments of broken shell that still survive in the ancient cultivation levels. The houses were variously constructed but were usually timber-framed and subrectangular, sometimes with low walls built of drystone work and with roofs of thatch sweeping down close to the ground.

Aerial photography and rescue excavation in advance of motorway construction have revolutionized our understanding of Iron Age settlements in Brittany over the last twenty years. Before that the only settlement feature widely known was the *souterrain* – an underground chamber tunnelled out from the granitic sand with access provided by one or two short shafts leading down from the surface. Hundreds of these souterrains came to light in the 1950s and 1960s, when Breton farmers first began to use tractors on a large scale and frequently found the ground giving way beneath the unaccustomed weight. The souterrains are puzzling structures. It is hardly likely that they were for shelter or refuge as was sometimes thought, though the suggestion that they were for the storage of grain seems more probable. But why store grain underground when there were perfectly serviceable above-ground granaries? Protection against raid is a possibility but there was surely more to it. Could it be that the Armorican farmers chose to place their grain below ground for religious reasons, believing that the deities of the underworld would protect the seed corn and maintain its fertility in the liminal period between harvest and sowing? In southern Britain, where at this time seed grain was stored in large pits, the local communities seem to have adopted this kind of belief: there is ample evidence that, after the grain had been taken out, propitiatory offerings were usually made. Belief in the power of the chthonic deities seems to have been widespread in Europe at this time.

While Pytheas may not have noticed the souterrains he could hardly have missed other manifestations of belief – the stelae, or pillar stones, scattered in their hundreds across the face of the countryside. Some were tall, standing several metres high, others were low and hemispherical. Most were carefully worked, as columns, or squared, or faceted pillars. Some were fluted and a few decorated. Taken together they are a remarkable demonstration of the strength of local cultural cohesion. In a few rare instances it is possible to show that stelae were associated with cemeteries but the vast majority are without archaeological context. Perhaps they marked some specially sacred place or a boundary, or indicated ownership. Whatever their meaning, Armorican communities were prepared to invest much energy in creating them, perhaps vying with each other to produce grander monuments much as, in the sixteenth century AD, their successors built ever more elaborate churches.

The decorated stelae, mostly concentrated in the Penmarc'h peninsula in the south-west corner of Brittany, form a remarkable group. The decoration is usually concentrated in two zones, around the top and bottom, while the column between may be fluted. The motifs adopted were normally running spirals and bands of Greek key though chevrons and diamond lattice were sometimes used. The tall fluted pillars with their bands of Greek key and running spirals at the top bear an uncanny resemblance to the columns of Greek temples. As a wild flight of fancy one might suggest that a Greek traveller arrived at Penmarc'h and there built a temple, perhaps in wood, to his protecting deity, and that it so impressed the locals that they copied its timber columns in stone. When such a hypothetical event might have taken place is limited by the dating of the decorated stelae which, on stylistic grounds, are usually assigned to the fifth century BC – a century or more before Pytheas. Tempting though this wild speculation might be, a far more likely explanation for the decorated stelae lies in the adoption of influences that were reaching Armorica from west central Europe in the sixth and fifth centuries.

We have already mentioned that in the fifth century the élites of west central Europe, in the Marne, the Moselle and to a lesser extent in Bohemia, enjoyed a period of spectacular cultural development. Luxury goods were exchanged with the Mediterranean world, especially with the Etruscans, and in the courts of the chieftains highly innovative craftsmen were developing a distinctive art style, which is generally now referred to as Celtic or La Tène art. To sustain such a system the élites must have been able to control the flow of raw materials, acting, as it were, as middlemen between the producers of the north and west and the consumers of the Mediterranean.

One of the routes along which goods were traded at this time was the Loire valley. The east–west movement seems to have been controlled by a centre of power focused on Bourges, in the vicinity of which the élites were buried with exotic bronze vessels and pottery imported from the Mediterranean. Bourges is crucially sited on the direct overland route linking the upper reaches of the River Cher, one of the tributaries of the Loire, to the upper reaches of the Loire, greatly shortening the journey to the Rhône and thence to the Mediterranean. It was no doubt through the élites of Bourges that bronze buckets and basins acquired from the Mediterranean were passed westwards in cycles of exchange, together with other less durable goods which no longer survive, eventually ending up in the hands of local chieftains in southern Armorica. The few known items, found by chance, hint at the kind of exotic trade goods that were reaching the Armoricans in exchange for what the locals had to offer – tin and some gold. Through these exchanges new decorative motifs common in the Mediterranean world were introduced to the Atlantic communities.

As the Marnian chieftains grew in power they too began to develop links with Armorica, using the traditional Loire route and possibly also the Seine, approaching Armorica by sea from the north. In the second half of the fourth century items of elaborate La Tène metalwork made in the Marnian workshops began to arrive in Armorica, there to be avidly copied by the local potters who now chose to adorn their elegant vessels with exuberant curvilinear motifs shocking in their novelty. Through the sherds of these pots found in archaeological contexts we can begin to glimpse this web of contacts that bound Armorica to the innovative centres of the Marne and beyond.

It was at just this time, when the new art styles were being introduced to the Armoricans and their potters were making their exquisite products, that Pytheas arrived in the peninsula. What he would have made of this barbarous local art we can hardly guess: he would have recognized echoes of designs used by Etruscans, but it was all very different transposed to the Atlantic periphery, there to be thoroughly reinterpreted by the native craftsmen.

We know little of the tribal organization of the Armoricans at the time when Pytheas arrived. He himself mentions that the westernmost tribe was called the Ostimioi which is usually taken to be the Osismii – the name used by Julius Caesar in 56 BC. Caesar also mentions two other tribes, the Veneti on the south coast in what is now the département of Morbihan and the Coriosolites of the north coast, now Côtes-d'Armor. These broad tribal groupings may well have existed in Pytheas' time but that they were not mentioned implies that Pytheas may have spent time only with the westernmost tribe. Caesar was particularly impressed by the Veneti who, in the first century BC, were, he tells us, in control of maritime trade. Their position, controlling the Bay of Quiberon and the estuaries to the west, would have suited them perfectly for this task. Their harbours would be the natural ports-of-call for ships coming up from the Gironde and for the traffic using the Loire, and from here the difficult passage westwards around the peninsula could be begun. Indeed it is quite possible that the ship carrying Pytheas from the Gironde stopped here *en route* for Ushant. The geographically favoured position of the coast of Morbihan ensured that it remained a focus for interregional exchange throughout prehistory, its pre-eminent position in the Neolithic and Early Bronze Age being dramatically displayed by the famous megalithic monuments of the Carnac region.

That the people of this coast were, by the Iron Age, experienced shipbuilders and sailors is certain and we can be reasonably confi-dent that the Venetic ships that so impressed Caesar had not changed much, if at all, since the time of Pytheas and probably for centuries before. Caesar's description of the Armorican ships he confronted in his famous sea battle with the Veneti in the Bay of Quiberon gives a vivid impression of the strength of the native vessels.

The ... ships were built and rigged in a different way from ours. Their keels were somewhat flatter, so they could cope more easily with the shoals and shallow water when the tide was ebbing; their prows were unusually high, and so were their sterns, designed to stand up to great waves and violent storms. The hulls were made entirely of oak to endure any violent shock or impact; the cross-beams, of timbers a foot thick, were fastened with iron bolts as thick as a man's thumb; and the anchors were held firm with iron chains instead of ropes. They used sails made of hides or soft leather, either because flax was scarce and they did not know how to use it, or, more probably, because they thought that with cloth sails they would not be able to withstand the force of the violent Atlantic gales or steer such heavy ships.

He goes on to say that the Venetic ships were much better adapted for the local weather conditions. They could weather storms easily and heave to in the shallow coastal waters fearing no damage when the tide went out and left them high and dry on the rocks. Although no part of an Armorican ship has yet been found, local vessels conforming closely to Caesar's description but dating to the Roman period have been recovered on Guernsey and in the Thames, demonstrating the longevity of shipbuilding traditions.

Pytheas would have become familiar with sturdy vessels of this sort in his travels around Armorica and on such a ship, leaving from one of the north coast ports, perhaps Le Yaudet, he would have resumed his journey northwards to Britain.

But what of the practicalities? How did he communicate and how did he pay his way? The language should not have been too great a difficulty, especially if he understood the rudiments of Celtic himself and was accompanied by a native speaker who could cope with the various dialects. As to payment – the word is too modern in its connotations: he would have made gifts in return for services. But what gifts? Given the distances he travelled, the commodities he and his entourage carried are likely to have been high value, low bulk. Gold and silver in the form of coin would have been highly acceptable, so too would fine cloth, coloured glass, unusual pigments, perfume and exotics of this kind. The chance that any of these items will have survived in the archaeological record is remote indeed and even if they did how would we ever be able to link them positively to Pytheas? The point is nicely made by the discovery of a gold stater, minted in the Greek town of Cyrene between 322 and 315, found at Lampaul-Ploudalmézeau in the north-west corner of Finistère only 30 km. from Ushant. The piece, in almost mint condition, was washed up on the beach, attached to the root of a piece of seaweed. Could it have been brought by Pytheas? We shall of course never know, but how tempting to think it was.

4

THE LURE OF TIN

The journey from the north coast of Armorica to Britain, a distance
of some 95 nautical miles, could have been accomplished within a
24-hour sailing. There are many safe and convenient landing places
along the Channel coast of Devon and Cornwall between Start
Point to Land's End. It is a coastline of deeply incised estuaries
created when, in the distant past, the sea-level rose gradually,
flooding the lower reaches of the river valleys and letting the ocean
creep further and further inland. This same kind of landscape can
be seen around the coast of Galicia in north-western Iberia where
the inlets are called 'rias' – a name now used by geomorphologists
to describe the phenomenon world-wide.

Wherever it was that Pytheas first landed on British soil it is
likely that he quickly made his way to the Land's End peninsula,
which, he would have learned from the Armoricans, was the island's
prime source of tin. He had, no doubt, heard vague stories of Britain
and its fabulous tin while living in Massalia. Now was his chance
to see the source for himself – probably the first Greek ever to do
so.

Rumours of the tin islands, known as the Cassiterides, lying
somewhere off the Atlantic coast of Europe, abounded in the
Ancient World. Herodotus was well aware of them but was prop-
erly cautious. Others were less so. Writing in the early years of the
first century AD, the Greek geographer Strabo was prepared to
assert that there were ten islands lying close together in the open
sea to the north of the Artabrians – a tribe who lived in northern
Iberia. They lay, he said, at a distance from the mainland greater

than the distance that separated Britain from the Continent. One was a desert but the rest were occupied by people who wore black cloaks with long tunics down to their ankles. They had belts around their chests and walked with canes. He thought they looked like the Furies in Greek tragedies. They were nomadic herders but had mines for tin and lead, which they traded, together with hides, in exchange for pottery, salt and bronze vessels.

Strabo, then, appears to have believed that the Cassiterides lay off the north coast of Iberia, but his geography is, to say the least, confusing and was made more so by Pliny, who, a little later, put the islands 60 miles west of Galicia. Both writers were simply repeating travellers' tales with all the scope for invention, exaggeration and error that the retelling allows. But Strabo adds one further detail. In former times, he says, Phoenicians from Gades had a monopoly of the trade and on one occasion when the Romans tried to follow a trading vessel to discover the route, the Phoenician captain deliberately 'drove his ship off course into shoal water: and after he had lured his pursuers to the same ruin he escaped on a piece of wreckage and received from the state [of Gadir] the value of the cargo he had lost'. But all to no avail, for eventually the Romans learned the secret.

Taken together these anecdotal scraps would seem to be referring to the tin sources of Galicia and the adjacent islands – the ultimate destination, as we have already seen, of the merchants using the Massaliot periplus. But it is *just* possible that mixed in with all this are echoes of other traditions of more distant journeys northwards from Iberia across the Bay of Biscay to the islands off the coast of Armorica or even, as some have suggested, to the Scillies and south-western Britain. All that can be said of this suggestion is that there is nothing in the sources (or in the archaeology) to give any support to the view or to the romantic idea, popular in the nineteenth century and still sometimes repeated today, that Cornwall was swarming with Phoenician traders.

The mining and export of British tin is mentioned in two ancient texts. The first is a brief and slightly muddled account given by Pliny the Elder in his *Natural Histories*, written in the late first

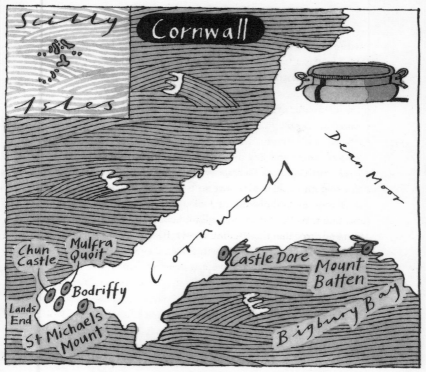

century AD. Pliny uses as his immediate source the Greek historian Timaeus of Tauromenium (*c.* 356–270 BC), who is known to have drawn extensively on Pytheas for details about the Atlantic. Although Pytheas is not directly credited in the citation in Pliny it may reasonably be assumed that he was the ultimate source. The second text is by Diodorus Siculus, a contemporary of Julius Caesar and Augustus, who wrote a massive compendium entitled *Bibliotheca Historica*, substantial parts of which still survive. He relied heavily on earlier books and is known to have used Timaeus. While he nowhere directly cites Pytheas there are sufficient similarities in some of his descriptions to suggest that, on Atlantic matters, his primary material ultimately came from Pytheas via the writings of Timaeus. To put all this another way, Pytheas' account was extensively used by Timaeus in the thirty or forty years after it was written and Timaeus was quoted sometimes with and sometimes without credit by Diodorus and Pliny about three centuries later. No wonder a few uncertainties have crept in.

What Diodorus says deserves to be quoted in full:

The inhabitants of Britain who live on the promontory called Belerion are especially friendly to strangers and have adopted a civilized way of life because of their interaction with traders and other people. It is they who work the tin, treating the layer which contains it in an ingenious way. This layer, being like rock, contains earthy seams and in them the workers quarry the ore which they then melt down to clean from its impurities. Then they work the tin into pieces the size of knuckle-bones and convey it to an island which lies off Britain, called Ictis; for at the ebb-tide the space between this island and the mainland becomes dry and they can take the tin in large quantities over to the island on their wagons. (And a peculiar thing happens in the case of the neighbouring islands which lie between Europe and Britain, for at flood-tide the passage between them and the mainland runs full and they have the appearance of islands, but at ebb-tide the sea recedes and leaves dry a large space and at that time they look like peninsulas.) On the island of Ictis the merchants buy the tin from the natives and carry it from there across the Strait of Galatia [the Channel] and finally, making their way on foot through Gaul for some thirty days, they bring the goods on horse back to the mouth of the Rhône. (*Hist.* 5.1–4)

Pliny's offering is briefer and more enigmatic:

The historian Timaeus says there is an island named Mictis lying six days' sail inwards from Britain where tin is to be found and to which the Britons cross in boats of wicker covered with sewn hides. (*Nat. Hist.* 4.104)

The description given by Diodorus is clearly taken from a carefully observed first-hand account and its evident fascination with tides is a further link to Pytheas, who is known to have offered comment on the subject several times. The promontory of Belerion can confidently be identified with the Penwith peninsula of Land's End, since the second-century writer Ptolemy calls Land's End by the variant spelling *Bolerium*. The name probably comes from the same root as the Celtic deity Belenos (an equivalent of Apollo), whose name means the bright-shining one. Perhaps the cliffs glinted in the sun or maybe a beacon fire was kept alight on the headland as a guide to sailors.

The rest of the account is a coherent description – friendly people used to traders, the method of tin extraction, the port-of-trade at Ictis and the transport of the tin across Gaul to the Mediterranean. If this is an accurate rendering of Pytheas' text it shows the quality of his observational skill.

The few lines offered by Pliny are more problematical. If Mictis is Ictis then what does 'six days' sail inwards from Britain' mean? And does the phrase 'where tin is to be found' qualify Britain in general or the island in particular? One perfectly plausible reading would be that the Britons carried tin from Britain in their hide boats to an island six days' sail from Britain 'inwards', that is, in the direction of the Mediterranean. This would place Mictis somewhere along the French coast between the Loire and the Gironde. Alternatively it could be telling the same story as Diodorus, in which case Mictis = Ictis but with a rogue distance of six days interpolated by error from somewhere else. Such uncertainties have provided unlimited scope for academic discussion over the last two centuries – an opportunity that needless to say has been avidly grasped by generations of scholars. Yet all that can safely be said is that the Pliny text is too garbled ever to allow certain interpretation.

Diodorus is quite explicit about the isle of Ictis. It lies off the British coast and can be reached by the carts carrying the tin at low tide. Here the foreign traders come to barter for it. From this description Ictis seems to be typical of sites chosen as centres for international trade throughout the world. Islands and promontories were safe places which all parties to the exchange could agree were extraterritorial. Here all who came were safe and could go about their business without political restrictions or harassment. Gadir itself was a classic island port-of-trade, so too was the island of Mogador off the coast of Morocco used by the Phoenicians in their trading ventures with Africa. People would come from considerable distances to these places at pre-arranged times, fixed by tradition and widely known, certain of finding someone with whom to strike a profitable deal.

But where was Ictis? On this subject debate has raged, each scholarly contestant eager to press the claims of his own favoured place, from the Isles of Scilly in the west to the Isle of Thanet in Kent. The most popular claimant is St Michael's Mount in Mount's Bay off the coast of Penwith. Physically it matches Diodorus' description, being cut off at high tide, and it lies conveniently close to the most prolific tin sources of the south-west. Another of its great advantages is that its commanding mass can easily be recognized from far out to sea – a quality which would have commended it to sailors unused to British waters. The only factor telling against it is that no relevant archaeological evidence has ever been found on the island, though this does not, of course, necessarily mean that none exists.

Another strong possibility is Mount Batten in Plymouth Sound. Today the site is a high rocky knoll, sadly diminished by quarrying, joined to the mainland by a narrow low-lying strip of ground. There is no positive evidence that it was ever an island at high tide but the linking strip has been much consolidated in recent times and there are earlier records of it being swept by waves, allowing the possibility that 2,300 years ago it might well have been cut off by the sea at high tide. As the site for a port-of-trade Mount Batten has many advantages, not least its sheltered position at the head of Plymouth Sound and the protected anchorages on each side, particularly along the Cattewater estuary to the north. It is also conveniently close to a prolific tin supply on the western edge of Dartmoor easily accessible via the River Tamar.

One of the strongest arguments in favour of Mount Batten is that there is indisputable archaeological evidence of intensive activity through much of the first millennium BC during which time an occupation deposit nearly a metre thick accumulated in the shelter of the rock. The layer of debris was packed with finds including a range of Late Bronze Age metalwork of the ninth to seventh centuries BC, ingots of copper and a large collection of Iron Age objects typical of the sixth to second centuries, most notably pins, knobbed bracelets of Continental type and a number of fibulae (safety-pin-type brooches). Two of these fibulae were of a type very rare in Britain but frequently found in Aquitania in south-west France. The collection of objects and pottery is quite remarkable. It shows that Mount Batten was visited time and time again, particularly during the period 900–100 BC, by people having access to an unusually wide range of artefacts of a distinctly cosmopolitan kind. It is exactly the kind of archaeological assemblage that one might expect to find at a trading port. This said, can we take Mount Batten to be the famous Ictis? The topography is more or less right, the date is right and the archaeology is right but still we cannot be positive – such is the frustrating nature of archaeology.

I confess to being biased in favour of Mount Batten, having spent two seasons excavating there, but to make a positive identification is to go beyond the scope allowed by the evidence. Mount Batten was a major port-of-trade at the time of Pytheas and it was the focus of interregional and international exchange. This much is clear, and at certain stages during its long life it was almost certainly the first port-of-call for vessels coming from the north coast of Armorica. At these times we can imagine pack-horses trudging across to the headland with their loads of tin and copper, and possibly some gold, from the Dartmoor edge while hide boats from Penwith arrived with yet more to prepare for the keenly anticipated annual visit of the Armorican traders.

Mount Batten was most likely one of a number of similar marts all along this coast, some large, some small. Their fortunes would have varied over time as the intensity and patterns of trading fluctuated. Given such a fluid situation can we ever hope to identify Ictis?

Diodorus twice mentions the transport of the British tin across Gaul. In the passage quoted in full above he says that the traders trans-shipped the tin to Gaul and then carried it by pack-horse to the mouth of the Rhône, a journey which took about thirty days. In a later section he adds that the tin was taken both to the Massaliots and to the city of Narbo. This suggests, but by no means proves, that two routes may have been in use, one from the mouth of the Loire upriver and overland to the valley of the Rhône, whence to Massalia, the other to the Gironde and along the Garonne and Aude to Narbo. In both cases the tin would have had to be shipped across the Channel and around, or across, Armorica to the Bay of Biscay and thus to the river estuaries. This part of the journey would most likely have been in the hands of Armoricans, unless that curious text of Pliny's actually means that some cargoes were trans-shipped to western Gaul by the Britons themselves in their hide boats. There is no reason why this should not have been so. The actual processes of transportation could well have been quite varied. For example, there is no need to suppose that all the cargoes were taken by sea around Armorica. A vessel leaving from Mount Batten may have preferred to off-load at a north Armorican port like Le Yaudet. In such a case the tin would have been carried across the peninsula via the valleys of the Léguer and Blavet to the south coast, to the vicinity of Lorient, before being put on board a local ship for the next leg of the journey. The overland journey of 140 km. would have saved a sea passage around the dangerous coast of Finistère of some three times the distance.

It must have been a time of great excitement for Pytheas at last to arrive at the source where the tin he had heard so much about was actually extracted. If the Diodorus text was based on his description, then it implies that he took a particular interest in the processes of extraction and, learning more, he can hardly have failed to have speculated about how the tin ore came to be formed in the first place.

In fact the process began about 280 million years ago when a molten mass from deep in the earth's core thrust upwards through layers of clays and slates, formed in the Devonian and Carboniferous age, to create a giant batholith 200 km. long which cooled and crystallized to become granite. In some places extrusions of molten rock pushed higher before they cooled and, after millions of years of erosion, now project through the surface to form the familiar granite uplands of Dartmoor, Bodmin Moor, and the moors of

St Austell, Carnmenellis, Land's End and Scilly: the warts along the spine of the batholith.

The molten extrusions greatly altered the sedimentary rocks through which they were forced, creating a metamorphosed aureole around them. As the granite cooled its crust the surrounding heat-contorted strata cracked and fissured and through these gaps hot, mineral-rich fluids poured, eventually to cool and crystallize, giving rise to an intricate network of mineral veins. As the temperature and pressure fell the different minerals crystallized out in turn. The first to solidify were tin and wolfram, then copper and finally lead and zinc. This means that the tin ores are usually found within or very close to the granite masses, the later-cooling metals being found progressively further away. In reality things are not quite as simple as that because on later occasions there were further phases of mineralization and sometimes old mineral lodes were opened up again to receive an intrusion of different minerals.

Mineralization was not evenly spread. There were some zones of mineral veins around each of the granite masses but the densest swarm occurs north and west of Carnmenellis Moor and around the western extremity of the Land's End granite. There were also quite significant deposits on the west side of Dartmoor.

The tin, which is our primary concern here, occurs as a stable oxide known as cassiterite (after the Greek word for the Tin-bearing Isles) and was often associated with iron-rich sulphides containing other elements such as arsenic and copper. These were less stable and quickly oxidized, the salts migrating in solution to form an iron-rich capping to the lode which had to be broken away to get to the tin. Cornish miners referred to it as 'iron hat'.

During the millions of years following the formation of the granite continuous erosion wore away the overlying metamorphosed rocks and exposed the uppermost part of the granite mass, eventually creating the moors we know today. Throughout this time the surfaces of the exposed mineral lodes broke away together with the surrounding granite and the fragments were washed into the nearby valleys. Cassiterite is very heavy and as the lighter minerals – the quartz, the feldspars and the micas – were washed away so the heavy cassiterite accumulated in a layer on the surface of the basal rock to form the 'tin ground', as the old miners called it. This process took place mainly in the early postglacial period when this part of Britain still enjoyed tundra conditions before the forests began to colonize the land. Over the following millennia, as the temperature improved, a variable thickness of sediments developed above these tin-rich gravels.

In the prehistoric period it would have been possible to get at the cassiterite either by quarrying out an exposed lode, digging as deep as safety allowed, or by collecting pebbles of the ore, easily distinguishable by their weight, from the 'tin ground' found at the bottom of cliffs of sediment exposed in the banks of fast-flowing rivers. Once it was realized that the cassiterite pebbles were mostly concentrated beneath the sediment, lying on the surface of rock, it would have been possible to identify likely spots and work to extract the ore in quantity, either by tunnelling in at the bottom of an exposure or by laboriously removing the overburden from the top to reach the tin-rich layer. The description of early mining given by Diodorus sounds very much like the process of digging cassiterite out of stratified valley deposits. Once the 'tin ground' had been reached the sand, grit and pebbles could be washed in a fast-flowing stream to remove the lighter material, leaving behind the heavy ore. In the nineteenth century experienced 'streamers' could do this by manipulating a wide-bladed shovel, full of the deposit, in a flow of water, retaining the cassiterite in the shovel while the lighter waste was washed away. This was called vanning. In such a way the concentrated ore could be amassed.

The process would also have exposed particles of gold – a metal which separated out of the cooling metal-rich fluid at about the same temperature as tin. Unlike the more reactive tin, the gold did not oxidize but remained in its native form. The gold was found in very small quantities, usually as tiny fragments each smaller than a pin-head. One nineteenth-century account describes how the tinners used to collect the particles and store them in a quill the end of which had been cut off and fitted with a small plug. They were allowed to keep what they collected for themselves, but if gold was thought likely to be found the miners were required to work for lower wages. The gleanings were usually fairly meagre, but very occasionally they could strike lucky, finding bigger pieces of which one of the most spectacular is the 59 gm. nugget found in 1808, now proudly displayed in the Truro Museum.

Once a sufficient quantity of cassiterite had been collected it would probably have been crushed by pounding and washed again with a stream of water to remove the lighter material, mainly quartz with a specific gravity of 2.5, leaving behind the heavy pure cassiterite, which has a specific gravity of about 5.4. The crushed ore was then mixed with charcoal and placed in a simple furnace. To reduce the cassiterite (SnO_2) to tin, temperatures of about 1000°C were required, which would have meant using bellows to raise the furnace heat. Once the smelting was over the 'prills' of tin could be collected and hammered together to form the knuckle-sized pieces that Diodorus mentions, or else melted in crucibles (tin melts at 232°C) and poured into simple moulds to make bun-shaped ingots.

No evidence of any tin workings of the time of Pytheas has been found in the south-west, but this is hardly surprising considering the intensive workings of the more recent period, particularly between the sixteenth and the nineteenth centuries when all the stream tin deposits were worked and reworked to make sure that every gram of commercially valuable metal was extracted. In this phase of intensive, large-scale activity all trace of earlier workings would have been destroyed. All that now remains is a small collection of ancient artefacts rescued over the last few centuries by miners and streamers curious about the ways of their ancestors. What survives is only a pale reflection of what there once was – much must have been destroyed or lost with little or no record – but the collection, nonetheless, provides an invaluable insight into the intensity and longevity of the earlier mining activities.

Among the objects that can be easily identified are a variety of bronze tools and weapons, including simple flat bronze axes, bronze rapiers and bronze palstaves of the second millennium BC as well as socketed spear heads and socketed axes of the Later Bronze Age, in use up to the seventh century BC. One find, made in the late eighteenth century at the Broadwater streamworks at Luxulyan, and recorded in the *Gentlemen's Magazine* for July 1795, comprised three sheet bronze cauldrons. The account tells how they were discovered on 28 March 1792, 'with their mouths upwards, and full of gravel about 28 feet under the surface of the earth'. The writer of the note speculated about their date, wondering if they were Phoenician or Roman. Although the vessels no longer survive, we can tell from the careful illustrations accompanying the report that they were, in fact, Late Bronze Age, dating to between the ninth and seventh centuries BC, and were of types found extensively along the Atlantic sea-ways from Iberia to Scotland. Cauldrons of this kind were often deposited as offerings to the gods. It is possible that here at Broadwater the Bronze Age 'streamers' were making an offering to the local deity, perhaps in thanks for allowing them to find a particularly rich deposit or in anticipation of better to come.

While finds of the Bronze Age are comparatively common in old tin works those of Iron Age date are much less so, but iron tools and weapons are less likely to have attracted the recent miners than the more exotic-looking bronze. It is likely that many were found but were simply thrown away. However, there is one find of outstanding interest – a fine bronze brooch now preserved in the Ashmolean Museum at Oxford together with a note recording that it was

found at Redmore nr St Austell in Cornwall under 6 ft of Peat & 20 inches of River Gravel. Beneath the sand lay another deposit of Peat 2½ feet in thickness which had been partly cut as fuel. Mixed with the cut blocks of this second peat deposit were the remains of a smelting hearth and pieces of Tin slag.

The brooch is of a distinctive type dating to the fourth or third century BC and could therefore have been in use at the time of Pytheas' visit. Its particular interest lies in its association with what appears to have been evidence of tin smelting.

A few other Iron Age finds have survived but they are of Late Iron Age date (first century BC–first century AD). The more spectacular include a bronze-bound wooden tankard found in 1851 in the Wheal Virgin works in the Pentewan valley and a decorated bronze collar from Trenowth in the Fal river valley found in 1802. Both came to light during the digging of 'tin ground' and it is therefore likely that they were deposited at the time when the tin was first being extracted two thousand years ago.

There is, then, plenty of evidence to suggest that the tin deposits were being extensively worked throughout the second and first millennia BC. By the time that Pytheas visited the area the industry already had a long ancestry.

Reviewing the long list of prehistoric finds recovered from the tin works over the last few centuries, what stands out is their quantity and their quality. The question which inevitably arises is whether all these valuable items could really be the victims of accidental loss or casual discard. It is surely unlikely. A more reasonable explanation would be to suppose that the majority were deliberately deposited to placate the gods of the underworld. Throughout this period there is a growing body of evidence to show that prehistoric communities held the chthonic deities in particular respect. These deities were believed to control essentials, such as a plentiful supply of water and the healthy growth of crops and animals. If one took what they offered it was important to repay them to maintain balance and harmony. So too with minerals. If the gods allowed you to discover and remove a prolific supply of cassiterite then they would expect gifts in return and only the foolhardy would neglect to satisfy divine anticipation. It is, I suspect, in this context of reciprocation and propitiation that such valuable objects were deposited, perhaps at the seasonal festivals when the ore-gathering was over for the year.

We have no real idea how the 'industry' was organized but there is no need to suppose that it was carried out by full-time professionals. A more likely scenario would be to see the collection and smelting of ore as a seasonal activity fitted into the slack periods in the farming year. Once the crops had been sown and the animals were out in their summer pastures there was time to get on with other activities. Those living near the coast might go to sea to fish while others might have spent their time digging for cassiterite or collecting copper ore. It was the kind of activity that could have been carried out while keeping an eye on the flocks and herds. The ore could have been worked where found, as was the case at Red Moor, where the brooch came from, or it could be taken back to the homestead and worked there. In other words the whole production may well have been essentially a cottage industry organized on a family or extended-family basis.

At the marketing level more complex organization would have been needed and here we may suppose that at certain designated sites, and at fixed times known to all, the individual producers brought their wares to take part in the seasonal exchanges and enjoy the festivities that no doubt accompanied them. One of these places was Ictis. Whether Pytheas visited the site himself at the time of a market or simply heard about it we can only speculate. But if the Armorican traders timed their journeys to the period of the markets, as seems likely, then we may quite reasonably picture him striding about the open-air bazaar observing the bartering in progress, well satisfied that he had achieved one of his aims and avid to learn all he could of how the tin was won.

Evidence that tin was being worked at the farming settlements comes from several archaeological excavations. At Dean Moor on the southern edge of Dartmoor a small cluster of stone-built huts was excavated in 1954–6 and shown to date to the Middle Bronze Age. Trodden into the floor of one of the huts was a pebble of cassiterite which had probably been collected from the stream tin deposit in the valley of the nearby river Avon. One of the other huts produced a small globule of tin with a vesicular surface typical of the 'prills' of metal that formed during the smelting process. Together these two tiny scraps suggest that the working of tin, albeit perhaps on a small scale, was one of the activities occupying the community living here.

Another settlement, at Trevisker, near Mawgan Porth on the north Cornish coast, also produced evidence of tin working. The farmstead at Trevisker had two main phases of occupation, the first in the Middle Bronze Age *c.* 1700–1300 BC, and the second in the Iron Age, probably in the second to first centuries BC. Of the Bronze Age settlement two small circular huts were excavated, both built of timber, together with parts of others and associated drainage ditches. Altogether the Bronze Age settlement produced more than twenty pebbles of cassiterite as well as lumps of slag, probably from bronze working. The Bronze Age community seem to have occupied the site on a permanent basis and to have gained their livelihood by raising domestic animals and growing crops on the fertile plateau above the River Menalhyl. It was in the river valley, only 2 km. away, that they probably collected the cassiterite, perhaps in the slack period of the farming year in late spring and early summer.

Dean Moor and Trevisker were both Bronze Age settlements dating to more than a millennium before the visit of Pytheas but the type of settlement and the farming regime that supported them did not change significantly over the next two thousand years.

One of the best-known settlements actively in use when Pytheas arrived in Cornwall is Bodrifty on the west slope of Mulfra Hill not far from Penzance. The settlement consisted of a number of circular houses (about ten were identified in the excavation) which at some stage were enclosed by a wall, creating a roughly circular 'pound' about 130 m. across. The houses themselves were quite small, with a living area 7–8 m. across enclosed by a thick wall faced with large granite boulders and infilled with rubble and earth. These walls would not have been very high and served to support the lower ends of the rafters of a conical roof covered with straw, reeds, heather or possibly turf. The floors were of earth with occasional paving stones and there was usually a central hearth. A single door, quite wide, with a paved threshold, provided access as well as being the only source of natural light. The huts would have been comfortable enough by local standards.

The hamlet seems to have continued in use for some time because several of the houses were found to have been rebuilt. Other houses were found outside the pound further up the hill scattered among small rectangular fields, altogether giving the appearance of quite a populous settlement. How many of the houses were in use at the same time is difficult to say but there were probably never more than a few families living on the hillside at any one time.

The small rectangular fields round about provided the permanent arable land of the settlement where the wheat and barley were grown. Sheep, cows and pigs were probably kept but no animal bones have survived in the harsh acidic granite soil. There were, however, seventeen spindle whorls, small perforated circular weights of pottery or stone, designed to give added weight to the spindles used for hand-spinning wool. A number of polished stones were also found which were probably used in dressing leather. Together the whorls and polishing stones help to fill out the picture of how the community lived and hint at the range of commodities, hides and woollen fabrics they may have produced in surplus for exchange.

The few potsherds that were recovered from the excavation were sufficiently characteristic to suggest that the settlement at Bodrifty had been occupied over a long period of time from the fifth to the second centuries BC. It is an amusing thought that one of the generations living at Bodrifty may well have heard news of this strange foreigner from the south who had turned up on an Armorican ship and was showing an unusual interest in the mundane and rather dreary business of extracting tin. The story might even have been told to children and grandchildren, acquiring all the various embellishments that elaborate folk traditions.

Had Pytheas taken time to explore the Penwith peninsula he would have seen many hamlets like Bodrifty nestling among their fields with the upland pastures beyond, and on the remoter hilltops the revered tombs of long-dead ancestors, built of massive stone slabs. Mulfra Quoit, Lanyon Quoit and Chun Quoit still dominate the landscape today. They would have reminded him of the megalithic tombs of Armorica and of the long and close relationships between the inhabitants of the two peninsulas.

There were other similarities too, most notably the sites that archaeologists conventionally call 'cliff castles'. These are promontories jutting out into the sea, separated from landward approach by one or more lines of banks and ditches. It used to be thought that such sites were defended refuges but more recently the possibility has been raised that they might have been sacred sites – liminal places at the interface between land and sea, perhaps serving also as guiding landmarks for mariners. The ancient Mediterranean was after all well supplied with 'sacred capes'. Cliff castles are a well-known feature of the coasts of Finistère and of Cornwall. Around the coasts of the Penwith peninsula alone seven cliff castles are known any of which Pytheas could quite easily have seen.

If Pytheas had travelled around Penwith he would have heard about, and perhaps even visited, the remarkable fortification in the centre of the peninsula known as Chun Castle. Chun was no mere peasant settlement. Its siting, on the summit of a hill, and its impressive walls would have been visible for miles around, proclaiming the status of its occupants. The actual settlement area is not large, barely 55 m. across, but it is surrounded by two massive granite-built walls 6 m. apart, each with a ditch outside. When nineteenth-century antiquarians made their first notes the inner wall originally stood to a height of 4 m. The single entrance, a gate 3 m. wide, was deliberately made more impressive by the outer defences being so arranged that anyone approaching had to pass along a narrow passage dog-legging between the two lines of fortifications. The effect would have been both to overawe the visitor and to place him at a distinct tactical disadvantage. Siting, size and design together contrived to endow the site with a sense of oppressive power.

Chun Castle was first described by a local archaeologist in 1769 and the first, rather desultory excavations were undertaken in 1895. Further work followed in the late 1920s, but the techniques used at this early date were not advanced enough to allow the archaeologists fully to understand the many phases of occupation and rebuilding that the internal buildings had undergone, from the time that the fortifications were first built, probably in the fourth century BC, until the site was last used as a convenient shelter in the eighth or ninth century AD. It is difficult, therefore, to say what the fortified interior originally looked like but it is likely that simple dry-stone buildings with inward-sloping thatch roofs lined the wall, facing inwards to the open courtyard where all the major activities of daily domestic life were carried out. Beneath the floor of one of the buildings, in what was probably an Iron Age layer, an oval ingot of tin was found, now much corroded, but measuring 20 by 17 cm. and 6 cm. thick. So much tin, some 5 kg., would probably have been of considerable value. Perhaps it was buried under the floor for safety, waiting to be taken to the next mart, only to be forgotten, but alternatively it could have been an offering to the deities to ensure the prosperity of the community.

A number of simple bun-shaped ingots like that found at Chun are known from Cornwall, most of them found in old tin works, but they are so simple in shape that they could have come from virtually any time in the prehistoric, Roman or medieval periods. Only the ingot from Chun Castle and another from the fortified Iron Age settlement at Castle Dore near Fowey can confidently be regarded as Iron Age in date.

Castle Dore, not far from St Austell Bay and the long deep estuary of the River Fowey, is an Iron Age settlement extensively excavated in 1936 and 1937. The main settlement area, some 80 m. across, was defended by a double bank and ditch, the outer defences diverging from the inner at the entrance to create a long corridor approach to the inner gate. Inside were a number of circular timber huts. The site seems to have been in use, but not necessarily continuously, from the fifth to first centuries BC and the finds from it suggest that it was a high-status site throughout, probably the residence of a local noble and his family and followers. The community had access to fine locally made pottery decorated with sophisticated curvilinear motifs and an unusual array of glass ornaments including two bracelets and four beads. Glass was rare, and presumably valued, in the Iron Age and although some glass is thought to have been made in Britain, much was probably imported either as finished artefacts or as raw glass metal. The two bracelets from Castle Dore are most likely to have been imports from the Continent brought in some time between the fourth and second centuries BC by traders from across the Channel. Trinkets of this kind, high in perceived value but low in bulk, were ideal trade goods, easily carried but much in demand, just the sort of thing that the Armoricans or Pytheas himself might have brought with them.

Of the ships themselves there is still no certain evidence but in 1991 a tantalizing discovery was made by a group of local divers from the South-West Maritime Archaeological Group, in the waters of Bigbury Bay. At the mouth of the River Erme where it enters the Bay is a dangerous partially submerged reef. Here, in some 7–10 m. of water, amid the broken rock, sand and kelp on the sea floor, divers found seven tin ingots in a single day's diving. Realizing the importance of their discovery they began a systematic search lasting for more than a year at the end of which more than forty ingots had been recovered and the position of each carefully plotted. The plot showed that the ingots were spread over a distance of about 26 m. along the north face of the reef and were quite clearly the cargo from a vessel that had foundered after being driven against the rocks by an adverse wind. Equally exciting were several pieces of ancient timber recovered in the same area. These were assumed to be parts of the vessel and it was confidently expected that a radiocarbon date would give a good indication of when the vessel went down.

The River Erme is one of the five main rivers that flow south from the granite massif of Dartmoor to the Channel, and Bigbury Bay is barely 25 km. (c. 16 nautical miles) from the Iron Age port of Mount Batten in Plymouth Sound. It is therefore quite possible that the Erme wreck was a vessel that was about to transport tin, from the Dartmoor fringe, on the short haul to Mount Batten where traders from Armorica might be expected to barter for it.

When the radiocarbon assessments arrived there was consternation. They dated the timbers to more than 4000 BC – far too early for the tin trade. The only reasonable explanation is that the timbers were nothing to do with the wreck at all but were from a much earlier forest which grew here in the Neolithic period, when the sea-level was much lower, and which was eventually submerged some time during the Bronze Age in a period of rising sea-level. These 'fossil forests' are known at several places along the coast and are sometimes visible at exceptionally low tides. It was a great disappointment but there remained the ingots. Most were of the general bun-shaped (or, more accurately, plano-convex) type which are impossible to date, but there were two that were more distinctive. They were H-shaped, with a thick cross branch, 8 cm. long by about 2.5 cm. across. In size and shape it would be perfectly reasonable to compare them to the astragalus of a cow (the astragalus is one of the metapodials in the fore and hind limbs). Could it have been small ingots of this kind that Pytheas was seeing and recording, and Diodorus several centuries later was writing about when he described the ingots as 'the size of knuckle-bones'? It is very tempting to think so, but such is the nature of archaeological evidence that so often we can never be entirely sure. Still, many Iron Age trading vessels must have foundered around the coasts of Devon and Cornwall – it can only be a matter of time before a well-dated example is found complete, let us hope, with its cargo of ingots.

5

THE ISLANDS OF
THE PRETANNI

From the viewpoint of the Mediterranean the British Isles were remote and mysterious. Rumours of these strange lands beyond the edge of the Continent abounded but there was little hard evidence about them or their inhabitants and even their name was in doubt. In the first century AD Pliny the Elder attempted to sum up the situation:

Across from this location Britannia Island, famed in Greek and in our own records, lies off to the north west, separated from Germany, Gaul, Spain and the greatest portion of Europe by a large interval. Albion was its own name when all were called the Britannias . . . According to Pytheas and Isidorus, the circuit is 4,875 [Roman] miles in extent. (*Nat. Hist.* 4.102)

Pliny then goes on to list by name and number the various islands making up the Britannias: 40 Orcades (Orkneys), 7 Haemodes (Shetlands?), 30 Hebudes (Hebrides), Mona (Anglesey), Monopia (Isle of Man), Riginia (Rathlin Island), Vectis (Isle of Wight), Silumnus (Scillies?) . . .

Pliny's text is not entirely clear but what he seems to be saying is that the entire group of islands off the Continental coast were collectively known as 'the Britannias'. Of these his contemporaries knew the largest as Britannia Island though the locals called it Albion. This would help to explain the confusion over names that pervades the other early texts and has tended to muddle the discussion ever since.

It begins with the short snippet which, as we earlier identified, was incorporated by Avienus in his poem *Ora Maritima*. The passage is describing what lies north of the Oestrymnides – here meaning Brittany: 'There is a two-day journey for a ship to the Holy Island – thus the ancients call it. This island, large in extent of land, lies between the waves. The race of Hierni inhabits it far and wide. Again, the island of the Albiones lies near . . .' Now there are several confusions embedded in these few lines. The first is that Avienus mistook the name of Ireland – (H)īwerō, later (H)īwerū (Iernē in Greek) – for the Greek adjective *hieros* meaning 'sacred', and to add to the muddle this concept – of the 'sacred' island lying near 'the island of the Albiones' – may have been further confused in his mind with the Sacred Cape and the Albiones of Iberia. But leaving all this aside, what his early unnamed source was telling him was simply that two islands, Hieriyo and Albion, would be encountered when sailing north from Armorica. Where this information came from is unclear but it is not impossible that Avienus culled the observation either directly or indirectly from the writings of Pytheas.

The earliest reasonably comprehensive description of the British Isles to survive from the classical authors is the account given by the Greek writer Diodorus Siculus in the first century BC. Diodorus uses the word *Pretannia*, which is probably the earliest Greek form of the name. The same spelling was also adopted by Strabo throughout his *Geographies* except in Book 1 where the 'B-' spelling is preferred. This apparent inconsistency could have been the result simply of a diligent scribe 'correcting' the spelling in the first book and then realizing that Strabo actually meant Pretannia and leaving the rest of the names unchanged. Since it is highly probable that Diodorus was basing his description on a text of Pytheas' (though he nowhere acknowledges the fact) it would most likely have been Pytheas who first transliterated the local word for the islands into the Greek *Prettanikē*. The original inhabitants would probably have called themselves *Pretani* or *Priteni*. The great Celtic scholar Kenneth Jackson argued that the former was the sound of the name current in the south of Britain while the latter pronunciation was used in the north. Interestingly, although in standard Latin the B- form became common, the original Celtic pronunciation still persisted and in Welsh the ethnic name *Pritani* eventually became the name of the island *Prydain* (Britain). The name *Priteni* remained in use in Roman Britain to describe the barbarians north of the Antonine Wall – the Picts – and the same word was used by the Irish, although, to confuse the issue still further, they pronounce it in the earlier Celtic form using Qu instead of P – thus *Quriteni*.

So, when Pytheas landed on the peninsula of Belerion he would have learned that the island was called Albion and that the people called themselves *Pretani*, which probably means 'the painted ones' or 'the tattooed folk', referring to their love of body decoration. This is not altogether certain because such a name, referring to physical appearance, would be a little unusual as an ethnonym (that is, the name by which a people call themselves), but would be more understandable if it was what others called them. So perhaps it was the Armoricans who called the inhabitants of Albion *Pretani* and Pytheas simply misunderstood, taking the word to be the actual tribal name, building further on his misunderstanding by naming their country *Prettanikē*. But perhaps we are being overcautious. It is simpler to accept that the local people were proud of their body painting and called themselves *Pretani*, for if we don't we would be admitting that our proud island name originated by mistake as a derisory nickname given to our ancestors by the forebears of the French! That would be too much.

Diodorus' detailed description of Britain, which we suggested above was most likely based on the account of Pytheas, deserves quoting in full:

Britain is triangular in shape, much as is Sicily, but its sides are not equal. The island stretches obliquely along the coast of Europe, and the point where it is least distant from the continent, we are told, is the promontory which men call Kantion and thus is about one hundred stades [19 km.] from the mainland, at the place where the sea has its outlet, whereas the second promontory, known as Belerion, is said to be a voyage of four days from the mainland, and the last, writers tell us, extends out into the open sea and is named Orkas. Of the sides of Britain the shortest, which extends along Europe, is 7,500 stades [1,400 km.], the second, from the Strait to the tip [at the north] is 15,000 stades [2,800 km.] and the last is 20,000 stades [3,700 km.] so that the entire circuit of the island amounts to 42,500 stades [7,900 km.]. (*Hist.* 5.21–2)

He then gives a brief sketch of the people and their lifestyle (to be considered below, p. 106) and goes on to say that he will offer a more detailed account of the customs of the Britons and other curiosities of the island when he describes Caesar's conquest. Sadly the surviving text ends before he reached that point. He does, however, conclude the section with the description of British tin, which we have already considered, and a discussion of amber, to which we shall come in the next chapter. Both of these detailed accounts were almost certainly taken from Pytheas.

Of all the ancient writers Diodorus gives the most coherent account of the general shape and size of the island, but Strabo and Pliny also offer some figures which both writers say they have taken from Pytheas. Strabo says that Pytheas claimed that the length of Britain was 20,000 stades and that the island was more than 40,000 stades in perimeter (here quoting Polybius) while Pliny quotes Pytheas as giving the perimeter of Britain as 4,875 Roman miles which works out at about 58,000 stades. The broad comparability of the figures given by Diodorus, Strabo and Pliny argues strongly that they must have been using the same source and that that source was Pytheas.

To turn all these measurements into something we can more easily understand it is necessary to indulge in a little simple mathematics. The stade was usually regarded as 125 paces but two systems of equivalents were in use. The more common allowed that there were 8 stades to the Roman mile but another used a slightly smaller stade, known as the Attic stade, so that the Roman mile was equivalent to about 8.3. This was the one preferred by Polybius. Leaving out various lines of calculation, the standard stade would thus be 185 m. while the Attic stade was 177.6 m. If Britain was 40,000 stades in circumference this would work out at

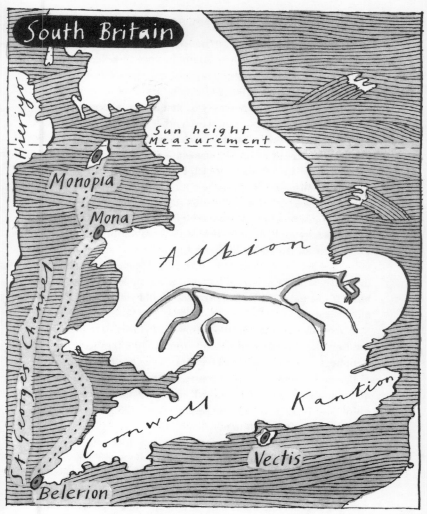

South Britain

Hieriyo

Sun height
Measurement

Monopia

Mona

Albion

St George's Channel

Cornwall

Kantion

Vectis

Belerion

7,400 km. or 7,100 km. depending on the stade length adopted. In fact, both figures compare remarkably closely with the estimate of the length of the coastline of Britain, given in the *Encyclopaedia Britannica*, as 7,580 km. But how could Pytheas have got so close? The only method he had of computing distance was to estimate how far they had sailed each day, taking account of sailing time moderated by his assessments of tides and winds and cross-checked by his measurements of north–south distance travelled, based on measurements of the sun's midday height at the solstice. Even for a highly experienced sailor the results are almost unbelievably accurate. The answer may simply be that all the inherent errors in his calculations tended to cancel each other out.

Strabo is, as usual, dismissive of everything Pytheas says. For example the 'length' of Britain opposite Keltikē, he argues, is 5,000 stades not the 20,000 stades which Pytheas quotes. But in this he completely misunderstands Pytheas for whom 'length' is the highly convoluted west coast from Belerion to Orkas, not the south coast as Strabo assumes. For comparability one must balance Strabo's 5,000 stades with Pytheas' 7,500 stades from Kantion to Belerion. In modern measurement Strabo estimated the south coast to be 900 km. while for Pytheas it was 1,350 km. Measuring the distance in a fairly straight line from a map it is a little less than 600 km. but if the actual coastline is closely followed Pytheas would be the more accurate.

In the same passage Strabo dismissed Pytheas' statement that Kantion (Kent) is some days' sail from Keltikē (France). At first sight he is right to do so. However, it may well be that the context of Pytheas' statement – that it took several days – was that he was describing his return journey from Kantion to Ushant at the western tip of Armorica, in which case several days' sailing would indeed have been required for him to reach Keltikē.

In taking a highly critical stance Strabo was following Polybius, whom he quotes with evident approval: 'many people have been led astray by him [Pytheas] . . . by his statement that he "traversed the whole of Britannikē accessible by foot" ' (*Geog.* 2.4.1). It might have seemed a ludicrous claim to Polybius but there is nothing inherently impossible in it. Indeed it presents the nature of Pytheas' expedition in a rather different light. Now we begin to see him as someone not simply content to explore the broad geography of the unknown but as a man with a real anthropological interest in the native inhabitants. It is entirely possible, indeed probable, that in his circumnavigation of Britain he made a number of overland journeys, always returning to the sea coast again to pick up a boat for the onward journey. In this way he would have acquired, and no doubt recorded, many details of the Britons and it was from this account that Diodorus selected the anecdotes he chose to repeat in his summary description of the island.

What route Pytheas followed in his exploration is a matter of guesswork, but from Cornwall we can suppose that he travelled northwards along the west coast in a series of short-haul voyages stopping off from place to place. A likely itinerary would have included south-west Wales, then along St George's Channel to the Lleyn peninsula and Anglesey before making for the Isle of Man.

That he stopped for a while on Man is a distinct possibility. We have already seen that at various points along his journey he made measurements of the sun's height which allowed him to calculate the distance he had travelled north from his home port of Massalia. These measurements were later translated into latitude by Hipparchus. One of the latitudes calculated from Pytheas' measurements was 54°14′. The parallel runs across the northern part of Ireland, just south of Armagh, passes through the centre of the Isle of Man and crosses northern Britain roughly through Scarborough. If, as seems reasonable, all his measurements were taken on his outward journey, so that he could track his progression northwards, then it is highly likely that this measurement was made on Man. Anyone using the western sea route along St George's Channel and the North Channel would have been attracted to the island by virtue of its convenient central position in the Irish Sea. Its safe anchorages and the opportunity to take on fresh water would have provided a welcome pause in the long sea journey.

After Man the onward journey through the North Channel would have led along the rugged west coast of Scotland and past its many islands, a route exposed at first to the full force of the Atlantic, but once past Tiree, into the Little Minch, gaining some shelter from the welcome barrier provided by the long run of the Outer Hebrides – Barra, Uist, Harris and Lewis. Somewhere on

Lewis his ship landed, very probably in the bay protected by Eye Pen at the site where the little town of Stornoway has since grown up. It was on Lewis that Pytheas took the third of his readings of the sun's midday height, allowing Hipparchus later to compute the parallel of latitude 58°13'. The latitude also crosses the extreme north of Scotland but it was to Lewis that Pytheas would have been drawn, both for its protected harbours and for the reputation it had gained for its remarkable megalithic monuments, which he would surely have wished to visit.

The suggestion that he took three measurements – Tregor, Man and Lewis, if we are correct in our identifications – at first sight appears to pose problems. To make the calculations of latitude, Hipparchus would have needed to know the exact height of the sun at midday on the midsummer solstice. If Pytheas had waited for the solstice, to set up his gnomon and measure its shadow, his journey from Ushant to Lewis would have taken over two years, to encompass the three solstices. This is by no means impossible, especially if he had chosen to spend time, as he claimed, exploring the land on foot, but there is another possibility. He need not have waited for the day of the solstice but could have taken his measurements before or after, so long as he was able to calculate the number of days to or from the solstice. This he would have been well able to do by reference to the constellations or by the length of day. Given these data Hipparchus' command of mathematical theory would have allowed him to work out the elevation at the solstice and from that the latitude. This said, it is quite possible that Pytheas tried to get as close to midsummer as he could and for this reason was prepared to extend his journey with lengthy expeditions on land.

From Lewis he probably sailed on, past Cape Wrath at the extreme north-western corner of Britain and then eastwards to the Orkneys, at that time a congenial place to stay for a while. 'There are', says Pliny, quoting Pytheas, '40 Orcades separated by moderate distances' – a remarkably accurate estimate if all the smaller islands are taken into account, suggesting particular knowledge.

Was Pytheas content simply to record what he had learned from

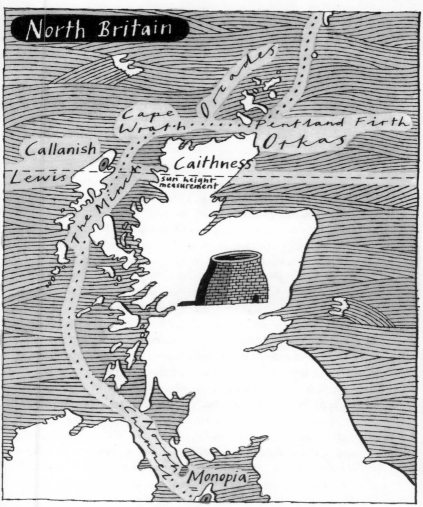

sailors encountered *en route* or did he make a thorough exploration for himself? The archaeological evidence shows, as we shall see later, that the islands were quite densely occupied by a stable population whose ancestors had built a remarkable series of burial monuments as well as alignments and circles of standing stones which were probably associated with the observation and worship

of celestial phenomena. For someone with Pytheas' scientific interests it would have been a fascinating place to linger to find out
what he could of the ancient wisdom of this remote region – so let
us leave him there for a while deep in his researches.

His journey from Cornwall to Orkney could have been accomplished within a few months but the solar observations he made on
the Isle of Man and Lewis, and his own claim that he had explored
much of the land of Britain on foot suggest that his progress
northwards may have been much more leisurely and was made up
of a series of short hauls from one port to the next, changing ship
wherever necessary. In this way he would have had the advantage of
travelling with ships' masters well used to the potentially dangerous
waters and who knew the vagaries of the sea and the safe havens.

The sea and its behaviour evidently excited Pytheas' enquiring
mind and he is known to have referred to it several times. Before
leaving on his northern journey his sailing experience had been
confined to the Mediterranean – a sea without significant tides.
Once he had left the shelter of the Gironde estuary he was in a
totally different world, experiencing tidal displacements of up to
15 m. in many places and always subject to the violence of the
Atlantic weather driving in from the west. It was a new and frightening world, bringing with it great excitements and mysteries.

The tides intrigued him. In the description of Ictis and the tin
traders he mentions the land bridge which appears at low tide, and
in parenthesis adds a further description of 'neighbouring islands
which lie between Europe and Britain' where at ebb-tide, as the sea
recedes, the islands take on the appearance of peninsulas. The
description sounds very much like the north coast of Armorica,
where the phenomenon is particularly dramatic, but it could equally
refer to the Channel Islands – and if so might give a hint of the
route by which Pytheas returned from Britain.

Pliny the Elder, in the contents to Book 2 of his *Natural History*,
lists Pytheas as one of the sources he consulted in gathering information on 'why the tides of the sea rise and fall and where
extraordinary tides occur'. Later he tells us that one of these extraordinary tides was claimed by Pytheas to be 'above Britannia

[where] tidal waters swell to a height of 80 cubits'. Another writer, Aëtius, whose work dates to the first century AD, notes that Pytheas thought that high and low tides were directly related to the 'fullness and faintness of the moon'. This same observation, however, was elsewhere attributed to Euthymenes, one of Pytheas' fellow Massaliots living a century or so earlier. It is quite possible that Pytheas studied his predecessor's writings before he set off, and he may have adopted some of Euthymenes' ideas in his own writings.

The observation, as reported by Aëtius, at first sight seems to be suggesting that Pytheas was somehow relating the half-daily tides to the phases of the moon: if so he would have been wrong. It is far more likely that what he was observing was that the tidal extremes – the spring tides – occur at full moon and new moon when the sun and moon are in line with the earth and together exert a greater gravitational pull on the ocean. Any of the maritime communities he came into contact with around the Atlantic coast would have been very well aware of the fact and it would have been a simple matter for Pytheas to have tested the observation for himself.

His claim that the tides 'above Britannia' reach heights of 80 cubits (some 35 m.) is way out if he was referring to the normal tidal range, but in the restricted seas of the Pentland Firth, between the north coast of Scotland and the Orkneys, the extreme tidal ranges exacerbated by low barometric pressure and gale force winds can produce mountainous surges. Waves up to 20 m. in height with great columns of spray going much higher are not unusual. And from time to time even more dramatic phenomena have been observed. In 1862 the island of Stroma, which lies off the north coast of Caithness in the centre of the Pentland Firth, experienced a tidal surge which surmounted cliffs nearly 70 m. high and swept right across the land. Stories of exceptional occurrences of this sort would have been preserved in the local folk traditions and readily recounted to travellers. Having experienced the fierce tidal race of the Firth for himself Pytheas would have been much inclined to believe such tales.

What kind of vessels Pytheas travelled in we can only guess. In all probability the tough oak-built boats of the Veneti, with their square-rigged sails of raw hide, were fairly typical of the vessels plying the Atlantic coasts and such craft may have served him for much of his journey, but there was also a quite different boat-building tradition in active use in the region – the skin boat constructed of hides stretched over a light timber skeleton. Hide boats of this kind were mentioned by Pliny when describing the transportation of British tin on its six-day journey to the trading island of Mictis. They are also referred to in the earlier source, the Massaliot periplus used by Avienus, in the description of seafaring around Oestrymnis in north-western Iberia.

No direct archaeological evidence has been found of these insubstantial craft and given their frailty this is hardly surprising, but one dramatic Irish find does throw a great deal of light on the nature of their construction. In 1896 a farmer ploughing his field at Broighter, on the shore of Lough Foyle near Limavady in Co. Derry, unearthed a spectacular hoard of seven gold objects which had been buried, probably in the first century BC or first century AD, as an offering to the gods. The group was dominated by a massive gold torque with buffer terminals heavily decorated with curvilinear La Tène decoration. There were also two twisted gold torques, two gold wire necklaces and two gold models, one of a cauldron, the other of a boat.

The boat is of outstanding interest not least for the accurate structural detail which it has to offer of these early craft. The shape of the hull suggests that the gold worker was modelling a hide boat. Inside were nine benches for the rowers to sit on and eighteen oars, each guided by a rowlock. At the stern was attached a large steering oar and towards the centre stood a mast with a yard-arm to take a square-rigged sail. Ancillary equipment included three forked barge poles and a grappling hook or anchor. The model is only 20 cm. long but the general proportion of the various fittings suggests that it is intended to represent a vessel some 12–15 m. long.

The Broighter boat, had it been built full size in withies and hide, would have been a sea-going vessel capable of long journeys over rough seas. The resilience and buoyancy of these craft were well known to Atlantic sailors and were vividly described by J. M. Synge, who enjoyed a number of hair-raising journeys in the currachs of the Aran Islands off the west coast of Galway early last century. Currachs are still in use there today though they are covered now not by hide but by tarred canvas.

The skin-boat tradition of the Atlantic was noted by several of the classical writers. We have already mentioned Pliny. At about the same time the poet Lucan was describing the weaving of osiers to form the wickerwork skeleton of the hull over which hides were stretched to create vessels used by, among others, 'the Britons on the broad-bosomed ocean', and the third-century writer Solinus, an avid collector of curious facts, refers to hide boats frequently crossing the Irish Sea. In the seventh and eighth centuries hide boats were also the principal means of travel for the Irish monks in their search for solitude. Adomnán's *Life of St Columba* written in the late seventh century gives a detailed description of these sea-going currachs with their large square sail hoisted to a mast set midships and with their rowing oars. This vessel also had a keel providing greater stability and rigidity. Another document, *The Life of St Brendan*, describes, in considerable detail, how Brendan and his friends set about building a currach with ribs and sides of wickerwork 'as is the custom in that country'. They covered the frame with oxhides tanned with oak-bark and caulked the joints with pitch, carrying with them on the journey butter to grease the oxhides. The craft was a large one powered by a sail set amidships, and was capable of carrying a crew of seventeen together with their provisions sufficient for fourteen days.

The tradition of large sea-going currachs persisted throughout the Middle Ages and became a source of some interest to the sea-going fraternity in more recent times. There is a particularly charming manuscript drawing of a currach, now in the library of Magdalene College, Cambridge. It was made in 1685 by Captain Thomas Philips and is entitled 'a Portable Vessel of Wicker, ordinarily used by the Wild Irish'. Clearly Philips was intent to communicate the rudiments of the craft to an audience unfamiliar with this still-surviving ancient shipbuilding technique.

To this tradition of sea-going hide boats the Broighter model belongs. The model is sufficiently detailed to leave little doubt that by the first century BC all the skills needed in building craft of this kind were already finely honed. Evidently Broighter comes comparatively late in a tradition going far back in time, possibly even to the Mesolithic period five millennia before. When Pytheas made his northern journey, the Atlantic seas through which he sailed must have been alive with hide boats of this kind. It is a reasonable speculation, therefore, that he would have travelled, for at least part of his journey, in such craft.

In his progress up the west coast of Britain Pytheas would have been aware that he was sailing between two large islands, especially when he passed through the North Channel between Kintyre and the coast of Antrim, and it is possible, but by no means certain, that his observations, made at this time, were the basis of the reference to 'Holy Island', and the race of Hierni who inhabited it, which was eventually incorporated into Avienus' poem *Ora Maritima*. There is no suggestion, however, that he ever landed on Ireland, though he would probably have heard many travellers' tales and might well have met Irish sailors in the British ports. The name for the Irish, Hierni, or, in later sources, Iverni, means 'people of the fertile earth' and is therefore quite probably the name by which the people knew themselves.

Later sources, such as Diodorus and Strabo, offer some comment on the inhabitants of Ireland. Strabo is graphically specific:

Concerning Ierne I have nothing certain to tell, except that the inhabitants are more savage than the Britons, since they are man-eaters, and since they count it an honourable thing when their fathers die to devour them, and openly to have intercourse not only with other women, but with their mothers and sisters as well; but I say this only with the understanding that I have no trustworthy witness for it.

Diodorus adds nothing to this, simply contenting himself with the bald summary that the people were wilder than the Britons, more promiscuous and indulged in cannibalism; both writers were probably using the same source.

It would be tempting to dismiss all this as fanciful stereotyping invented to characterize a distant barbarian people about whom nothing was really known. As such it would be typical of its kind. It is an interesting speculation that, though Pytheas is not identified as the source, the story may have originated from him, and Strabo's comment, that he has no trustworthy witness, might be a back-handed jab at his source.

The description is worth looking at in a little more detail. The sexual behaviour which Strabo mentions, while somewhat alien to a Greek or Roman, simply reflects a different set of social values which may have been widespread among the Celts. In a later description of the Britons of south-eastern Britain, Caesar suggests that much the same values were held there. 'Wives', he says, 'are shared between groups of ten or twelve men, especially between brothers and between fathers and sons.' None of this can be taken entirely on face-value, and it is unwise to try to reconstruct social systems from such anecdotal and potentially biased evidence, but it does seem that the rules governing sexual bonding may have been more complex in Britain than in Mediterranean society.

Nor should the suggestion of endocannibalism be entirely dismissed. Much later, in the fourth century AD, St Jerome came upon a group of Attacotti, probably from Ireland, in his travels in Anatolia and was shocked to find them eating someone. Anthropological studies in many parts of the world show that cannibalism was practised well into modern times. Thus, what at first sight appear to be grotesque inventions to give memorable substance to little-known barbarians might in reality contain some germs of accurate anthropological observation.

Pytheas' intriguing statement that he 'traversed the whole of Brettanikē accessible by foot', which Strabo quotes, following Polybius, is, no doubt, something of an exaggeration, but there is every reason to suppose that he explored as much as possible of the countryside accessible to him from the western ports that he put into. How extensively he reported what he saw in *On the Ocean* we shall never know but two samples survive through Strabo and Diodorus.

Strabo, as was his custom, wrote off Pytheas' observations as fanciful. Describing the people who 'live close to the chilly zone' he says that

of the domesticated fruits and animals there is a complete lack of some and a scarcity of others, and that the people live on millet and on other herbs, fruits and roots; and where there is grain and even honey the people also make a drink from them. As for the grain, since they have no pure sunlight, they thresh it in large store houses having first gathered the ears together there, because [outdoor] threshing floors are useless due to the lack of sun and to the rain.   (*Geog.* 4.5.5)

Diodorus provides rather more detail:

Britain, we are told, is inhabited by tribes who are indigenous and preserve in their way of life the ancient customs. For example they use chariots in their wars . . . and their houses are simple, being built for the most part from reeds or timbers. Their way of harvesting their grain is to cut off only the heads and store them in roofed buildings, and each day they select the ripened heads and grind them, in this manner getting their food. Their behaviour is simple, very different from the shrewdness and vice that characterize the men of today. Their lifestyle is modest since they are beyond the reach of luxury which comes from wealth. The island is thickly populated, and its climate is extremely cold . . . It is held by many kings and aristocrats who generally live at peace with each other.   (*Hist.* 5.21.4)

Diodorus does not identify Pytheas as his source, but the details of the method of harvesting would seem to have come from Pytheas' description and it is quite probable that the rest does too. Strabo was, after all, being highly selective, taking only those details which he believed made Pytheas look like a liar.

The description of the harvesting method is particularly interesting since it implies a very specific system. The growing corn would have been grasped in one hand just below the ears and cut, below the hand, with an iron reaping knife, leaving the stalks still standing in the field. There would have been several advantages to this procedure. It would reduce the volume of material to be carried from the field and the volume requiring storage before threshing and it would leave the stalks and weeds of cultivation – prolific in pre-chemical farming – to provide animal fodder for a succession of animals, first for cows, then sheep and finally for pigs. Sheep could get at the lower growth left by the cows while the pigs would root through what was left, breaking the ground up and helping to mix in the copious supply of manure deposited during the gleanings. At the end of the process the field was ready for ploughing. Meanwhile the ears of corn were stored in granaries and threshed when needed, the threshing waste providing additional food for animals.

There is archaeological evidence for much of this. Small iron reaping hooks are frequently found in Iron Age settlements and rectangular granaries with raised floors, built on a framework of four or six vertical timbers, are found throughout southern Britain within settlement enclosures and hillforts. There is also fairly clear evidence from the remains of charred crops that the grain was being cut high in the fields – the argument resting on the fact that the lower-growing weeds of cultivation were usually absent.

One tangible feature of Iron Age agriculture was the storage pit – some as much as 2 m. deep. They are found over much of south-eastern Britain, and were probably used to store the threshed seed corn during the period between the harvest and the next year's sowing. Experiments have shown that if pits of this kind are well sealed at the top and air is excluded grain stored in them will survive well for at least a year with little deterioration and no loss of germination. The fact that no mention is made of this in the texts might suggest that Pytheas did not visit the south-east of the country where the practice was prevalent, but there are many reasons why he might not have referred to it or why the later writers might have chosen to leave it out of their summaries, so the omission is not significant. The reference to grain being threshed indoors because of the climate could really apply to any part of Britain. Most Iron Age farmsteads in the south-east that have been excavated on a large enough scale are composed of several circular buildings. One of these would have served as the main house but the others may have had separate social or domestic functions, accommodating wives or the young men of the community or used for cooking, weaving or threshing. Over most of southern and eastern Britain the houses were, as Diodorus remarks, built of timber with the roofs, and possibly walls, covered with reeds or straw.

Most prehistoric communities will have developed ways of manufacturing alcoholic drinks through fermentation. Barley was widely used and as early as 2000 BC the dead were accompanied in their graves by large pottery beakers (hence the archaeological name Beaker Folk) which probably contained beer of some kind for their journey to the afterworld. Several classical writers refer to beer and mead drunk in quantity by the Celts of Gaul before Italian wine took its place as the élite drink in the late second century BC. Interesting archaeological confirmation for this comes from a rich chieftain's burial found at Hochdorf near Stuttgart. Here the dead man was laid out in great splendour in a wooden burial chamber accompanied by a range of very elaborate equipment including a large bronze cauldron of Greek manufacture. In the residues recovered from the cauldron scientists identified pollen remaining from the honey, which had been used, with the fermented grain, to make the mead that was poured into the cauldron at the time of the burial, just before 500 BC. The Britons whom Pytheas met two centuries later were still brewing their drink in this time-honoured way.

Strabo's mention of millet grown as a crop is puzzling since millet does not grow in Britain. Some commentators have sought to get over the problem by suggesting that Pytheas may have used the word to describe oats with which he was otherwise unfamiliar. While this is possible, oats are far closer in appearance to the other cereals he would have known and not at all like millet. From the context of the word, he is referring specifically to the 'chilly zone' and is distinguishing it from other regions 'where there are grain and honey . . .' It may be that he is describing a particularly extreme location where there were no cultivated cereals and people ate seeds, fruits and roots, yet archaeological excavations in the extreme north of Britain do not bear this out. Iron Age sites in the Hebrides, Caithness, Orkney and Shetlands have all produced evidence of barley cultivation. At Bu Broch on Orkney grains of emmer wheat were recovered in addition to barley, while at Crosskirk Broch on the north coast of Caithness oats were also grown. But Crosskirk may provide the clue, for here one of the more prolific plants found in the sealed archaeological layers was Fat Hen or White Goosefoot (*Chenopodium album*) – a plant we would now regard as a garden weed but one that was widely valued in the prehistoric period as a food since its seeds are a rich source of oil and carbohydrate. Fat Hen was among the seeds found at Bu Broch on Orkney. That it was sometimes a significant part of the Iron Age diet is well demonstrated by the stomach contents of the famous bog-bodies from Denmark, which contained high percentages of Fat Hen and Dock, both plants producing seeds with a high oil content. Fat Hen is not unlike millet in some respects. It has a small round seed 1.5 mm. in diameter and black in colour, while the seeds of millet, also round, are about twice the size and pale yellow-brown. The closest similarities between the two lie in the way in which the seeds cluster together. Another possibility is that Pytheas mistook Brome Grass (*Bromus secalinus*) for millet. It has a seed rather like a small oat but is rare in Iron Age archaeological sites in the north.

Of the fruits and roots which he mentions in general terms there are many to choose from. The rhizome and young shoots of bracken are highly nutritious and widely available. Crowberry and rose hips were collected by the occupants of Bu Broch and there are several fine seaweeds to be found, not least the tangy 'dulse' still to be bought today in the markets of western Ireland.

Information about the use of the chariot in warfare, noted by Diodorus as one of the ancient customs that still persisted among the Britons, could have been derived from Julius Caesar's *Commentaries* (also known as his *Gallic Wars*). Caesar was particularly impressed by the British chariots in warfare, saying that they combined the mobility of cavalry with the staying power of infantry. He had every cause to appreciate their versatility since his armies faced a British force fronted by 4,000 chariots. But Diodorus does specifically say, after his general description of Britain, including the mention of the chariot, that he will give a detailed account of the Britons and their country later when dealing with Caesar's campaigns. This book was never written, or at least does not survive, but that he made the comment gives a strong hint that he was drawing on two different traditions, deliberately keeping them separate.

It would have been quite possible for Pytheas to have seen chariots in Britain. Small, light, two-wheeled vehicles drawn by a pair of small horses yoked together are well known from Iron Age burials found in Yorkshire dating from the fifth to the third centuries BC and horse gear and metal chariot fittings are widely distributed over most of the country. If he had travelled along the Yorkshire coast on his return journey he might even have seen a burial ceremony with one of the local élite being interred with his dismantled vehicle. Elsewhere in the country, though chariots were in operation and may even have featured in burial rites, they were not actually placed in the graves with the dead.

In his journey up the west coast of Britain Pytheas would have encountered many different communities with different social traditions reflected in the varying layouts of their settlements. He would also have been aware of the changing styles of architecture as his journey progressed. In the Penwith peninsula of Cornwall, as we have already seen, there were hamlets of scattered circular huts with occasional strongly built élite residences such as Chun Castle. If he had stopped in south-west Wales he would have seen a landscape of ditched and banked enclosures, quite strongly defended, with impressive entrances each containing two or three circular huts and several rectangular granaries. Further north, on the Isle of Man, the houses were much bigger, large roughly circular structures up to 20 m. across with their interiors divided into zones by concentric circles of posts supporting roofs of branches covered with turves. These structures would have been barely visible, appearing only as low mounds, but identifiable by the wisps of smoke escaping through a gap in the roof above the central hearth.

Once into the North Channel the landscape would have changed dramatically to one dominated by rocks, steep cliffs and long narrow inlets. Exposed to the full force of the North Atlantic gales, this was not a country of many trees. Instead of timber and turf the local communities built in stone, available there in plenty. By the time of Pytheas' visit thick-walled stone houses were coming into fashion, replacing an earlier tradition of multi-celled houses of low visibility largely sunken in the ground. The circular houses were upstanding statements of the community's permanence and of their claim on the land. They served as family dwellings but they were also territorial markers. Later, by the first century BC and first century AD, the circular house tradition was to develop into buildings of almost tower-like appearance called brochs. The brochs differed from the simpler stone houses of the earlier period in that their walls were much higher and thicker and contained cells with passageways and staircases leading to the parapet. The roof of the house within was now completely hidden by the high walls. But these were developments to come.

The sort of house that Pytheas might have visited, or indeed stayed in, on Orkney would have been like Bu Broch near Stromness, excavated in the 1980s. It was a circular house with an internal floor area about 10 m. across, protected by a wall nearly 5 m. thick. The interior was divided by stone slabs into a central area dominated by a large hearth and a series of compartments opening off around the inside of the wall. Some of these individual rooms would have provided privacy – they were quite large enough to sleep in – while others would have been used as storage space.

The community here made good use of the local resources. We have already mentioned the barley and wheat that were grown nearby and the crowberries and rose hips collected from the wild. There was also a plentiful supply of protein from cattle, sheep, pigs and wild deer, and from fishing, which brought in plaice from inshore and medium-sized cod from further out in deeper waters. To this were added shellfish, birds and no doubt birds' eggs. The diet, insofar as it can be deduced from the archaeological remains, was balanced, varied and healthy.

In his long sea journey north, broken by excursions on land, Pytheas would have learned much of the ways of the people and of their myths and legends. Nothing of this comes down to us directly ascribed to him nor is there much of this kind repeated by Strabo or by Diodorus. Yet there is a possibility, certainly no more than that, that a garbled fragment, embedded in Avienus' *Ora Maritima*, may have been derived from Pytheas. As it now stands, in a particularly turgid and overblown passage, better paraphrased than translated, Avienus tells us that if one sails from Armorica to 'where the air of Lycaon grows stiff' (by which he means the far north where it freezes) one would enter the land of the Ligurians now empty of inhabitants (Ligurians here simply meaning ancient indigenous populations). Because of constant battles with Celts the fields are abandoned. The indigenous peoples moved to the land they now occupy, a rocky place with rugged cliffs and threatening mountains thrusting to the sky. They live here still fearful of the sea because of the ancient danger but sometimes when all seems quiet they venture down to the shore again.

It is a particularly interesting fragment apparently recalling a historical event. But the geography is elusive. If 'north from Armorica into the freezing regions' is taken literally it would lead us to the west of Scotland or just possibly the north-west of Ireland. Both would fit the description of a rocky place with cliffs and mountains bordering the sea. It is a tempting speculation but it can be no more than that.

Yet in the story there is a vague echo of a folk-tale, preserved in the Irish vernacular literature in a series of stories known as *The Mythological Cycle*, which tells of the five successive groups of invaders who occupied Ireland before the ancestors of the present inhabitants arrived. The last of the group, the Tuath Dé Danann (the Peoples of the Goddess Danann), were eventually overcome by the Sons of Míl and were driven into the hills and the fairy regions. How much of all this had threads of real history woven into it and how much was pure invention we shall never know.

Any people seeing daily the monuments of long-distant ancestors around them could be forgiven for making up stories to explain them. The need to 'understand' the past and all its manifestations is deeply felt: only in doing so are we able to control it. A hundred generations ago people created myths from the fragments of folk memories passed down to them – today we turn to archaeology. It is a comforting conceit to think of Pytheas on Orkney visiting in wonder the great megalithic monuments – the Stones of Stenness, the Ring of Brodgar and the awesome tomb of Maes Howe, all even then nearly three thousand years old – and trying to reconcile them in his tidy scientific mind with the local myths and legends he was hearing, told around the comfort of the hearth at night.

ULTIMA THULE

The very words 'Ultima Thule', echoing across the centuries, carry with them the magic of the remote, the far distant, the very limit of the known world. Thus it was that the poets and philosophers of the early Roman Empire – men such as Seneca and Virgil – came to use the phrase. Aware, no doubt, of the tedious academic debates surrounding the geographical reality of Thule, picked over in the works of Polybius, Strabo and others, the many who came after were content to use Thule simply as a convenient romantic image. Like all good romantic images it hovered on the boundaries of the unreal, creating a *frisson* of excitement – of unresolved adventure. For all this we have Pytheas to thank. But before we begin to explore the reality which may lie behind the stories that Pytheas brought back it is helpful to move on a few centuries to see how the early medieval historians viewed the distant north.

The Venerable Bede, writing in the eighth century AD, clearly believed Thule to be Iceland, when he described travellers arriving in Ireland from Thule with stories about the sun being visible for several nights on end during midsummer. Educated men, knowing the classics, could, of course, have made up such things but there is no reason to doubt the first-hand experience of Bede's informants.

The next century provided even more conclusive proof. About AD 825, an Irish scholar-monk, Dicuil, working in the Frankish courts of Charlemagne and Louis the Pious, wrote his famous work *De Mensura Orbis Terrae*. Dicuil was evidently a skilled geographer and astronomer and had access to a wide range of classical texts and other sources, some no longer surviving. One of these was the verbal report of a group of clerics who had been to Iceland thirty years before, in AD 795. In retelling their adventure he prefaces it with a brief discussion of Thule as seen by the Latin writers Pliny, Isidore of Seville and Solinus, who all believed Thule to be a remote island north-west of Britain. Then comes the story:

It is now the thirtieth year since some monks who dwelt upon that island from [1 February until 1 August] told me that not only during the summer solstice but also during the days near that time, towards evening the setting sun hides itself as if behind a small hill, so that there is no darkness for even a very short time; but a man may do whatever he wishes, actually pick the lice from his shirt just as if it were by the light of the sun; and if they had been on top of the mountains the sun probably never would have hidden from their eyes. In the middle of that short period of time it is midnight in the middle of the earth; and so I believe that, on the other hand during the winter solstice, and during the few days around that time, dawn occurs for only a brief time in Thule, that is to say, when it is midday in the middle of the earth. Therefore those are lying who have written that the sea around Thule is frozen and that there is continuous day without night from the vernal to the autumnal equinox; and that *vice versa*, from the autumnal to the vernal equinox there is perpetual night. Those monks who sailed there during a time of year when naturally it would be at the coldest and landed on this island and dwelt there, always had alternate day and night after the solstice; but they found that one day's sail from it towards the north the sea was frozen.

Dicuil's careful reporting of the monks' experiences is important in a number of ways. Since it in no way glorifies the voyage, it implies that travelling to and from Iceland was not uncommon and had probably been going on for some while before 795. Moreover, that they had chosen to make the outward journey in midwinter would suggest a certain confidence borne of experience – though foolhardy bravado is not unknown among monks! And if they were to survive the winter weatherproof buildings of stone and turf must surely have been available immediately on arrival. Together these considerations point to a tradition of visits going well back in time.

The accurate observation of solar events enabled Dicuil to dismiss the errors and misunderstandings in some of the classical texts. He would specifically have had in mind Pliny's statement that on Thule there were 'continuous days for six months as well as continuous nights', a statement Pliny attributes to Pytheas. Although Dicuil is correct in refuting this it is not too difficult to understand how the idea arose – a matter to which we shall return.

That there were, indeed, Irish monks settled on Iceland is well established, for when the Viking settlers began to arrive from Norway about AD 860 they found the books, bells and croziers that the monks had left behind as they fled the island in advance of the large-scale pagan settlement. There is, however, surprisingly little archaeological evidence for pre-Viking settlement although a few place-names, incorporating the word *papa* – meaning a priest – are suggestive of early Christian sites. Exactly when the first Irish monks arrived in Iceland is uncertain but Dicuil says that the monks began to adopt the practice of putting to sea in hide boats, in search of the solitude of remote places, sometime around AD 700. If the existence of Thule was already suspected it is likely that the island would have been sought out early in the wanderings of the *peregrini*.

Possible evidence of earlier visits is extremely meagre. All that can be brought forward is three Roman coins of the late third century. Two were found on an ancient settlement site at the head of Hamarsfjord on the south-east coast of the island, one in 1905 and another in 1933, mixed up with material of the Viking and later period. The third coin was picked up from the surface of a sand dune in the same region in 1923. While it would be quite reasonable to explain these finds as much later imports, brought in by the Irish monks or the Vikings as curios, it remains an outside possibility that they were carried on Roman ships exploring the North Atlantic five centuries or more earlier. The question cannot be resolved on the evidence available but there is nothing inherently improbable in the Romans sending an expedition to locate Thule.

That the Irish were able to sail to and from Iceland in the eighth century AD in their large hide-covered currachs – even in midwinter if they chose – raises the question of how far back in time people from the Atlantic coasts of Ireland and Britain were making such voyages. There is no real difference between the ocean-going cur-rachs described in the *Life of St Brendan* and the vessels represented by the Broighter gold model dating to the first century BC and it is likely that boats of this kind, with a square-rigged sail and provision for a team of rowers, were already well established at least as far back as the Late Bronze Age when the volume of traffic along the Atlantic sea-ways appears to have been intense. Thus it would have been technically possible to make journeys from Britain or Ireland to Iceland in the first millennium BC – but, that said, what might have induced men to submit themselves to the hazards of the ocean and how would the pioneers have been confident of finding land?

The answer to the second question lies in the heightened senses that mariners develop for navigating. Using every sign available to them – the direction and magnitude of the swell, the colour of the water, floating detritus, distant cloud formation, even the smell of the land carried far out to sea by the offshore breezes – they build up their own cognitive map of the ocean.

One of many signs, used by sailors throughout the world, was the direction of flight of migrating birds. Observed over a number of years consistent patterns would soon have been recognized and it would have been no great intellectual leap to deduce that the birds were moving from one territory to another. Thus, by following their course across the ocean, it would have been a reasonable supposition that new lands lay out there to be found.

The principal migratory routes used by the coastal species of western Europe lie along the west coast of Britain, in spring leading northwards via the Faroe Islands to Iceland and thence to the Arctic. To the communities living on the Atlantic coasts of Scotland and on the Hebrides the annual migration pattern of birds, such as the Whooper Swan with its loud bugle call and unmistakable V-formation, would have been a sign of the onset of spring, punctu-ating the calendar, but their passage was also a regular reminder that somewhere along the route they were signing, far to the north, lay land.

Birds as a navigational aid feature in the saga told of the Viking

Flóki, who sailed from Norway in AD 874 with three ravens on board, intent on reaching Iceland. He set out westwards, keeping on the latitude he believed would lead him to the island. After several days at sea, sighting no land, he released the ravens one at a time. The first flew back the way they had come towards Norway, the second, after circling, returned to the ship, but the third flew straight ahead. With renewed confidence Flóki set the ship in the direction the bird had taken and eventually made a safe landfall on Iceland's south-east coast. While this happy story may have been the embellishment of the scribe who wrote down the saga in the thirteenth century it at least shows that the use of birds in navigation must have been entirely credible at this time. An even more dramatic case is the story told of Pedro Cabral, who, on the morning of 22 April 1500, having taken an unusually wide westerly swoop on his course down the west coast of Africa *en route* to India, spotted an unusual flight of birds. Believing them to be land birds he changed course, following them to the west, and by evening had discovered Brazil.

If the birds flying northwards along the west coast of Britain convinced the local people of the existence of land somewhere out there in the ocean, we have still to consider what may have motivated them to set out in search of it. The trite answer, of course, is the spirit of adventure, and this is difficult to gainsay. To explore is a human characteristic unrestricted by time – after all, we have the example of Pytheas himself. But what might have been the mind-set of those who lived in the north in the third, second or early first millennium BC? There is ample evidence that by the third millennium people had taken ship to Shetland and carried their domesticated animals and seed corn with them, and that early in the first millennium BC skilled metallurgists were sailing around the islands, from Aran off the Galway coast of Ireland to remote Shetland, carrying beeswax, refractory clay and bronze scrap with them to set up shop and cast whatever bronzes the local communities desired. Sea travel was normal and essential. All this is well attested in the archaeological record.

A little earlier, around 3000 BC, the local communities had

The Circle of the Bear (Arctos)

Iceland

The Cronian Sea

N

Faroes

Shetlands

Orkneys

Ultima Thule   Lewis   Scotland

developed a refined interest in astronomy, building circles of
upstanding stones on Lewis and Orkney and spectacular chambered
tombs such as Maes Howe on Orkney that were aligned with the
setting sun on the midwinter solstice. People with these abilities,
who had acquired through experiment and long observation an
intimate knowledge of celestial phenomena, were astronomers in
their own right. Perhaps it was they who were first led north by the
V-formations of the Whooper Swan to explore the behaviour of
the sun and the constellations – tentative exploratory probes at first
with many failures, until at last land was reached and the route
established for others to follow. It is one of the frustrations and
fascinations of archaeology that on matters of this kind we are
seldom likely to find conclusive evidence. But anyone who has
looked at the sophistication of Maes Howe and considered the
dominating belief that drove people to erect the Stones of Stenness
or the circles and alignments of Callanish cannot fail to wonder at
the innovative power of the local élites at this time. If ever the
moment was right for exploration this was it.

When Pytheas arrived in these waters in the fourth century BC the drive and excitement of this remarkable phase were long since spent. The monuments remained for all to see and the folk memories that explained them were there for the hearing, but the moment had passed. One can imagine the excitement that Pytheas, the astronomer, must have felt in seeing these ancient monuments, in many ways as remote in time for him as they are for us. He would have listened avidly to the stories and tried to penetrate the ancient wisdom. This is hardly in doubt because it is evident from his records that he had spoken to people who had sailed north to Thule and had observed the wonders of the place first-hand. Could he have resisted the temptation to see for himself the land where the sun does not sleep?

Before we return to the scraps of reported anecdotes which might contain the clues we must try to get into the mind of Pytheas, to understand the world as he saw it.

He would have conceived the earth as a sphere lying in the centre of another sphere – the celestial sphere – which mirrored in its poles, equator and tropics those of the earth within. Because the sun was carried around the earth (it was believed), with the revolution of the cosmos the shadow of a vertical staff – a gnomon – describes the arc of a circle. Since the further north one goes and the hours of daylight in summer lengthen, the circumference of the arc becomes longer until the point is reached beyond which the shadow at the summer solstice would describe a complete circle within a 24-hour period. Posidonius used the word *perioikoi* to describe people who might have lived here – the word simply means 'dwellers around' – though it was generally believed to be far too cold for human life. The tropics (from the Greek *tropoi* meaning turning-points) were the most extreme positions of the sun at the summer and winter solstice. Here the shadow is cast north for one half of the year and south for the other half. North of the Tropic of Cancer the shadow always lies to the north as far as the Arctic Circle (the Circle of the Bear) beyond which the shadow completes the circle. The Circle of the Bear (*arktos*) was so named because beyond it the stars forming the constellation of the Great Bear never dip below the horizon and so are always visible.

The celestial equator, the two tropics on either side and the circle of the ever-visible stars were conceived of as circles on the celestial sphere which were projected on to the terrestrial sphere within.

All of this would have been within Pytheas' understanding, but he had no concept of measuring parallels in degrees. It was Hipparchus of Nicaea who, in the mid-second century BC, was to establish the system of parallels of latitude we use today, located at one-degree intervals between the equator and the poles. In this system, assuming the celestial sphere is 360°, the summer tropic – the Tropic of Cancer – is at 24°N and the Circle of the Bear is at 66°N. Hipparchus spent most of his working life at his observatory in Rhodes but gathered data from earlier writers, among them Pytheas, whom he evidently considered to be highly reliable. With this, as we have seen, he established several northern latitudes in his projected system of parallels.

Hipparchus understood the mathematics necessary to convert distances travelled on the face of the earth, and the elevation of the sun at the midsummer or midwinter solstice or the maximum number of hours the sun was seen, into parallels expressed in the form of degrees. But Pytheas, a hundred and seventy years earlier, had no conception of this. He would have been well aware, of course, that the sun's shadow at midday on the solstice lengthened as one went north and from this would have been able to work out its elevation above the horizon. He would also have noted that the number of hours of sunlight at the summer solstice increased the further north he travelled but would almost certainly not have had the means to make accurate measurements of this. Nor would he have been able to measure the distance he had travelled except by the rule of thumb that a ship could travel so many stades in a day. Given these limitations, the measurements that Pytheas recorded, and those which Hipparchus had available for his calculations, are most likely to be sun heights. Hipparchus converted them to degrees of latitude but Strabo seems to have preferred to express latitude in stade distances and length of longest day. These he would probably have calculated from the data provided by Hipparchus. The measurements which Pytheas took and their calculated equivalents are:

	height of sun (cubits)	longest day (hours)	distance stades north of Massalia	° latitude
Thule		21–2		66°
Shetland	>3	19	9,100	61°
Lewis	4	18		58°
Isle of Man	6	17	6,300	54°
Tregor	9	16	3,800	48°
Marseille	?	15½		43°

The two most northerly of these we have still to discuss, but before doing so we need to consider a few facts about Iceland that will be directly relevant to the extent of Pytheas' travels. Iceland lies largely between the latitudes of 63° and 66° while the Arctic Circle – the southernmost point of total solstitial sunlight – at 66° 32′ just touches the northernmost extremity of the island at Rifstangi.

The circumpolar traveller Vilhjalmur Stefansson, who knew Iceland well from first-hand experience, gave an account of the facts that he thought were most relevant to the Pytheas debate. The variable geomorphology of the north coast of the island imposed limitations on what could be seen of the midnight sun. There were some promontories from where the sun could be observed to skim along the northern horizon for several days in succession but at the head of some of the deeper fjords the sun could not be seen at all, or not the whole of it. Exactly what was observed therefore depended on where the observer was. Another point to bear in mind is the size of the island. From its extreme northern tip on the Arctic Circle to the south coast is a distance of 340 km., more than three degrees of latitude. Over such a distance there were significant changes in the hours of daylight at midsummer. Official timetables in Reykjavik in the south-west corner give the times of sunset and sunrise even on the longest day, but, this said, the amount of ambient light can be such that even here you could see to 'pick the lice from your shirt' at midnight. In recognition of this the laws of the country allow that lighthouse beacons be turned off for three months each year. In other words, although the sun does set, a visitor might be excused for speaking of a three-month-long day.

With these preliminaries now established, we can turn to the collection of observations ascribed to Pytheas.

The first, and in many ways most contentious text is the one we have already considered, in which Strabo repeats what Pytheas said about the food eaten by the 'people near the chilly zone', mentioning among other things honey. This description is prefaced by one of Strabo's customary disparaging remarks:

Concerning Thule, our information is even less clear because of its remoteness, as this is the place writers say is the very farthest north of all named locations. That the things Pytheas said about it and other places in those parts are fabrications is clear from his description of areas familiar to us. He lied about most of these, as I have already said, so it is clear he is an even worse liar about more obscure places. (*Geog.* 4.5.5)

Leaving aside Strabo's value judgements, there is no need at all to suppose that the description of the food of the inhabitants of the 'chilly zone' has anything to do with Thule. Indeed Strabo's phrase 'the things Pytheas said about it *and other places in those parts*' offers a clear separation between Thule and the inhabited zone. The point may seem self-evident but it has to be made here because some commentators have mistakenly used the mention of crops and bees to argue that Thule could not be Iceland. The two are unconnected even in the mind of the muddled and hostile Strabo.

Strabo seems to be content to accept that Thule was 'the very farthest north of named locations'. Elsewhere, and without criticism, he reports that Pytheas claimed Thule to be six days by sea north of Britain 'and near the congealed sea'. The word congealed is usually taken to mean solidified, i.e. frozen. The same six-day journey is mentioned by Pliny, who, in a separate section, adds that off Thule (which he calls here Tyle) one day's voyage brings you to 'the Congealed Sea which some call "Cronian"'.

Six days' sail from Britain – but from where in Britain and by what route? From the Orkneys via the Faroes to Iceland is about 500 nautical miles but if the journey is routed from Orkney via the Shetlands to the Faroes and thence to Iceland an extra 80 nautical miles would be added. To accomplish the distance in six days would have meant covering between 85 and 100 nautical miles in each 24-hour period, which would have required speeds of 3.5 to 4 knots. This is well within the range of what is possible given fair winds and favourable currents, though under less favourable conditions the journey might have taken much longer. The extra day's journey to the 'Congealed Sea' fits well with the sea conditions around Iceland, for a single day's sailing up the east coast of the island could reach drift ice even in the summer. The report has a clear echo in Dicuil's account more than a thousand years later, when he says that 'they found that one day's sail from it [Iceland] towards the north the sea was frozen'.

Understandably, the celestial phenomenon reported by Pytheas created much interest among his Mediterranean readers. There are two basic observations. The first concerns the length of the day:

during the solstice days when the sun comes nearer to the top of the world, because of the confined course of light, the earth beneath has continuous days for six months as well as continuous nights in winter when it is remote in the opposite direction. (Pliny, *Nat. Hist.* 2. 186)

Pliny repeats the same point again later:

. . . Thule where, as I have said, there are no nights during the solstice when the sun is passing through the sign of Cancer and also no days during the winter solstice. Some believe this is true for six continuous months. (*Nat. Hist.* 4. 104)

The same information is repeated by Martianus Capella writing in the fifth century AD but the likelihood is that he took the paragraph direct from Pliny's *Natural History*.

We have already seen that when Dicuil came across this passage in Pliny (and possibly in other texts) he simply wrote it off as lies, realizing that it was incorrect. Strictly this is true, but the overall effect of the sun's trajectory throughout the summer is to light up the sky even when it sets, to such an extent that it allows the Icelandic lighthouse keepers their three months of inactivity. An observer of these remarkable effects can surely be excused the exaggeration of writing of many months of continuous day. It may also be that Pytheas was more circumspect in his record and is loosely interpreted by Pliny.

Another source of considerable interest is Geminus, who is thought to have studied in Rhodes in the middle of the first century AD, where he wrote a textbook on astronomy, *Introduction to Celestial Phenomena*:

It would appear that Pytheas the Massaliot was in fact present in these regions [the north]. He says among the observations recorded by him in *On the Ocean*: The barbarians pointed out to us on several occasions the place where the sun lies down. For it happens around these places, that the night is extremely short: two hours in some, three in others, so that after the setting, although only a short time has elapsed, the sun straightaway rises again.

He goes on to explain that further north there is a 24-hour day and that under the poles there are six months of daylight and six months of darkness. His knowledge of astronomy is thorough and he has the confidence to extrapolate to make statements about places he has never visited. The 21- or 22-hour day could have been observed anywhere in southern Iceland, which extends as far south as 63°N. At first sight this would seem to imply that Pytheas or his informants had actually visited Iceland but unfortunately we cannot be sure from the extant text whether the whole piece is a direct quote from Pytheas or whether the full quotation is the single sentence that the barbarians pointed out where the sun lies down, the rest of the information about the length of the night being added by Geminus based on his own calculations. As so often happens with ancient texts, what at first seems to be a clinching certainty dissolves into ambiguity as soon as it is critically scrutinized.

The second piece of astronomical information ascribed to Pytheas concerns the Arctic Circle. The observation is summarized by Strabo:

The Massaliot Pytheas says that the very last regions are those around Thule ... near which the summer tropic is the same as the Arctic Circle. (*Geog.* 2.5.7)

The same fact is repeated in a work on astronomy written by Cleomedes, probably in the first or second century AD:

Concerning the island of Thule, in which men say that Pytheas the Massaliot philosopher was actually present, the report is that the whole summer circle is above the earth, it being the Arctic for them.

These are rather obscure statements but what they imply is that the summer tropic (i.e. the Tropic of Cancer) is the same distance north of the equator as the Arctic Circle is south of the North Pole, the one at 24°N (0° + 24°), the other at 66°N (90° −24°). The Arctic Circle just touches the northern extremity of Iceland.

I have left until last the most intriguing of Pytheas' observations of Thule, preserved for us by Strabo who at this point is quoting Polybius. After a general dismissive statement – that many people have been led astray by Pytheas – Polybius gives various examples of things he cannot accept, ending with Thule:

and those parts where neither earth was in existence by itself nor sea nor vapour, but instead a sort of mixture of these rather like a marine lung in which ... the earth and the sea and all things are together suspended, and this is as if it were a fetter of the whole, existing in a form impassable by foot or ship.

Strabo then adds:

The thing like a lung he himself [Pytheas] had seen, but other things he spoke of from hearsay. (*Geog.* 2.4.1)

Understandably this paragraph has given rise to much discussion. While it would be possible to interpret the text in a metaphysical way, as an allegory of the edge of existence where nothing is as it seems and the elements of earth, water and air merge into one, this is contrary to what we have come to expect from Pytheas' accurate and rather dispassionate style. It is simpler, perhaps, to see it as an attempt to describe the frightening conditions that can occur at sea on the edge of the Arctic among the blocks of drift ice where the freezing ocean coagulates into a heavy ice-sludge and a thick freezing fog descends, merging the air and the viscous water into one. At such a time the sense of complete dislocation – from time and tangible reality – easily slips into panic. One such occasion is captured by Pierre Loti in his famous novel *Pêcheur d'Islande*, based on the life of fishermen from Pampol in northern Brittany who spent the summers catching and salting cod off Iceland:

It was daylight, the everlasting day of those regions – a pale, dim light, resembling no other; bathing all things, like the gleams of a setting sun. Around them stretched an immense colourless waste . . . all seemed transparent, ethereal, and fairy-like. The eye could not distinguish what the scene might be: first it appeared as a quivering mirror which had no objects to reflect; and in the distance it became a desert of vapour; and beyond that a void, having neither horizon nor limits.

It is usually thought that the name 'Thule' comes from the Greek *thoule* or *thule* of unknown meaning but one possibility is that it derives from *tholos*, which may be interpreted as 'murky', 'clouded', 'indistinct'. This would fit well with Pytheas' description of the ethereal approach to the land.

And what of Pytheas' 'marine lung' (*pleumōn thalassios*)? There has been much ingenuity spent over its explanation. Perhaps the sluggish rise and fall of the 'congealed sea' reminded Pytheas of the ocean respiring, or perhaps he was likening its motion to that of a giant translucent jellyfish (*pleumōn* is the word used by Plato for jellyfish); if so it is a powerful and appropriate metaphor for an experience that must have stayed vivid in his mind for the rest of his life.

And so we have come to the end of Pytheas' testimony of the northernmost seas. The two questions which remain are whether Thule was really Iceland and how far along the route Pytheas himself ventured. As to the first, there are three schools of thought: that Thule is indeed Iceland, that it was Norway and that it was Shetland. It will be clear from the way I have presented the evidence that I belong to the Iceland school. To me the evidence seems unassailable. The six days north from Britain (not east to Norway), the day of twenty-two or twenty-three hours, the Arctic Circle and the place where the sun sleeps, and the frozen sea – all these things point to Iceland. To Dicuil, writing in the ninth century, there was never any doubt. He was influenced, of course, by his own interpretation of the classical texts but could it perhaps be that he was also familiar with the name Thule, or some variant of it, from an Irish tradition of sporadic visits, going back into prehistory?

Those who favour Norway follow the Scandinavian writer Fridtjof Nansen, whose book *In Northern Mists*, published in 1911, relied heavily on the assumption that the description of crops and bees referred to Thule, which could not therefore be Iceland; but, as we have seen, Strabo's text deliberately separates Thule from the cultivated region. Nor could one reach the frozen sea in a day's sailing even from the extreme north of Norway.

Those who support Shetland do so partly because they think it inconceivable that Pytheas could have made a more distant exploration and partly because Tacitus evidently believed Shetland to be Thule. In describing the circumnavigation of Britain by the Roman fleet in AD 85 under the command of his father-in-law Julius Agricola, Tacitus says, 'At the same time it discovered and subjugated the Orkney Islands, hitherto unknown. Thule was sighted but no more' (*Agricola* 10). In this belief he was followed by Ptolemy in the second century, but these statements are based on nothing but an understanding that Thule lay north of Britain.

There is, however, one scrap of evidence to support the view that Pytheas may have been to Shetland. He recorded a place where the shadow of the sun was less than 3 cubits high. From this Hipparchus calculated a nineteen-hour day and a latitude of about 61°. This would coincide with the extreme north of Shetland (though the Norway school would also point out that this is roughly the latitude of Bergen).

If, then, we accept that the weight of evidence strongly points to Thule being Iceland the question remains whether Pytheas was ever there.

The view, held here, that Iceland had been visited, if sporadically, throughout the later part of the prehistoric period, at least from about 1000 BC, would allow that knowledge of the island was preserved in the folk traditions of the north of Britain. On the Hebrides, the Orkneys or the mainland Pytheas could have picked up stories of this fabulous island six days' sail to the north. He could have learned about the congealed sea and it might have been from the comparative comfort of Orkney or Shetland that 'The barbarians pointed out . . . on several occasions the place where the sun lies down'. Such information may have been among the 'other things he spoke of from hearsay'. He was certainly a collector of stories. And yet 'Pytheas says he glimpsed all the northern part of Europe as far as the limits of the cosmos,' says Strabo, and again: 'The thing like a lung he himself had seen', while Cleomedes, writing of the island of Thule in the second century AD, could add, 'in which men say that Pytheas the Massaliot philosopher was actually present'. There is a strong tradition, then, that Pytheas claimed to have travelled the six days northwards to the edge of the cosmos to see the astronomical wonders of Thule for himself.

Let us imagine a possible scenario. From Lewis, the north coast of Scotland or, more likely, Orkney, Pytheas takes a local ship to Shetland and makes for the extreme north of the islands to measure, or estimate, the height of the sun at the solstice. Estimate is more likely given the approximate measurement – 'less than 3 cubits' –

which he recorded. Standing on Hermaness Hill, perhaps, at the northernmost point of the island of Unst looking northwards across the Skerries of Muckle Flugga and Out Stack, he would have thought over his monumental journey from his home port of Massalia, where the sun's maximum height was more than 10 cubits, to the reading he was now getting of less than 3. He had in fact travelled through eighteen degrees of latitude and had penetrated further north than any Mediterranean before him. And yet there were those stories he had been told by the men of the north of the great island of Thule far across the open ocean to the north where the sun slept and the sea froze. For all his heroic travels he had not yet reached the limit of the cosmos. Perhaps he returned from the hill to take shelter in the little homestead at the head of Burra Firth near the present holding of Stackhoull to think over these things. Would a man who had come so far and faced so much danger and discomfort turn back now, only six days away from the edge of the world, never to witness its celestial miracles? Surely not. Perhaps he returned south, crossing from Unst to Yell and to Mainland, making for one of the principal homesteads of Shetland, the walled settlement on the island in the loch of Clickhimin next to the present town of Lerwick. Clickhimin has been excavated and is now an impressive monument, its complex of walls reflecting building activity and use spanning a thousand years from the Late Bronze Age to the Christian era. Its persistence and comparative wealth owe much to its favoured position commanding, as Lerwick was later to do, the Bressay Sound – a safe anchorage protected from the east by the island of Bressay.

It may have been here that he found men prepared to take him on the last leg of his journey. A community like this was used to the ocean. They farmed the land but without the harvest from the sea their lives would have been meagre. The archaeological layers at Clickhimin have yielded quantities of whale bone and while some may have come from stranded creatures it is likely that whaling was a normal part of life: so too would have been deep sea fishing for cod and the like. Of the boats we have no evidence, but lack of good timber on the exposed Shetlands means that the inhabitants would have made their vessels of a light wooden frame-

work covered by hides. There is ample evidence, in the archaeological layers, of the pegs and scrapers needed to work the skins.

All this may sound disastrously insubstantial as a way of travelling across the North Atlantic but on the other side of the ocean
the Inuit have long been building ocean-going skin boats known as
umiaks. These vessels, 10–15 m. long, can carry weights of up to
two tons and frequently take between ten and thirty people, yet the
vessels are light enough to be carried by two men. As to perform-
ance, a high-sided, flat-bottomed umiak drifts rapidly before the
wind and, so long as the joints are well greased, takes aboard little
water. For manœuvrability and resilience the American whalers of
north-western Alaska, at the end of the nineteenth century, adopted
the umiak in preference to the wooden whale-boat. With three
thousand years of boat-building tradition behind them we can be
reasonably certain that the Shetlanders were competent to build
safe, sturdy craft capable of crossing to Iceland.

And so, one morning in early summer we can imagine Pytheas in
the company of local sailors setting out along Bressay Sound and six
days or so later arriving off the south-east coast of Iceland. Later
they would have sailed northwards around the east coast, landing
perhaps at Rifstangi just inside the Arctic Circle. They might even
have timed the visit so as to be there on the summer solstice. Then
there would have been the one-day journey north into the frozen
sea before at last turning for home. The whole trip could have been
accomplished within three or four weeks. Back in the comfort of
Clickhimin Pytheas might have rested a while, content to wonder at
the marvels he had seen.

It is, as we have said, an imaginative scenario – a fairy story
perhaps; a product of wishful thinking. Yet, returning firmly to the
hard evidence available to us, journeys of this kind from Orkney and
Shetland were perfectly within the technical capabilities of the people
at the time and may not have been a rare occurrence. The details of
the far north, recorded for the first time by Pytheas, are scientifically
coherent and were observed by someone. The only question, then, is
whether Pytheas, having got so far, would have been content with
hearsay. He claims not. Let us take him at his word.

7

THE MAGIC OF AMBER

In Greek mythology Phaethon was the headstrong son of Helios, the sun, and Clymene, daughter of Oceanus. One day, to demonstrate his divine parentage, Phaethon persuaded his father to let him drive the four-horse chariot carrying the sun across the heavens but the wonder of it all was too much for him and he lost his nerve. The horses ran out of control, veering far too close to the earth, searing it with the sun's heat, creating the Libyan desert and threatening to consume everything. Zeus, seeing that the world was in danger of total destruction, flung a thunderbolt at Phaethon, instantly killing the youth, whose body fell to earth near the River Eridanus, sometimes identified as the Po. Here his sisters, the Heliades, buried his badly burned body. Such was their grief that they sat on the banks of the Eridanus and mourned. Four months later they were changed into poplar trees but their tears, now the sap of the trees, continued to flow, dropping into the river and turning into amber – a substance which therefore combines the intense colour of the sun with the clear transparency of tears. The Greeks called it *electrum* after the name of the sun, Elector – the Shining One.

A charming story but Herodotus will have none of it:

I do not admit that there is a river called by barbarians Eridanus which discharges itself into the sea towards the north, from which amber is said to come . . . For in the first place, the name Eridanus shows that it is Greek and not barbarian, and made up by some poet; in the next place, though I have diligently enquired, I have never been able to hear from any man who has himself seen it, that there is a sea on that side of Europe. However, both tin and amber come to us from the remotest parts.

In this statement the circumspect Herodotus rejects without comment the belief that the Eridanus was the Po in favour of the more popular belief that it was a mysterious north-flowing river. Other identifications were also canvassed – that the Eridanus was the Rhône or even a river in Iberia. Some believed that amber, brought down by the Po, was washed up on islands in the Adriatic, called the Electrides, while another favourite myth was that amber was shed by trees growing on inaccessible rocks at the head of the Adriatic. More exotic origins were also on offer – that it was washed up on the capes of the Pyrenees by the ocean in turmoil, that it flowed from the mountains of Britain, that it was the consolidated urine of lynxes, that it was the tears of birds shed in India, or that it was the sap of poplars gathered in the pools of the mythical Garden of the Hesperides in the Western Ocean by the daughters of Hesperus.

The various myths current in the Greek world, disparate and imaginative though they are, have several things in common – the understanding that amber could be fossilized resin from trees, that it has some association with the Western Ocean and that the Po valley and the head of the Adriatic feature in some way in the story of its acquisition. There is some truth in all these beliefs. By the time that Herodotus was writing, in the fifth century BC, it was clear that amber was coming from the north, probably from the shores of the largely unknown Northern Ocean, and was being transported, via the river system, to the Mediterranean. We now know, from ample archaeological evidence, that one of the principal routes led from the coast of Jutland, where amber was exposed, along the River Elbe and its tributary the Vltava, then overland to the Danube and the Inn, via the Brenner Pass, to the Po valley and thence to the head of the Adriatic. Another route began at the Gulf of Danzig, close to the rich amber supplies on the south-eastern shores of the Baltic Sea, and led along the Vistula, across the North European Plain, through the Sudeten Mountains to the River

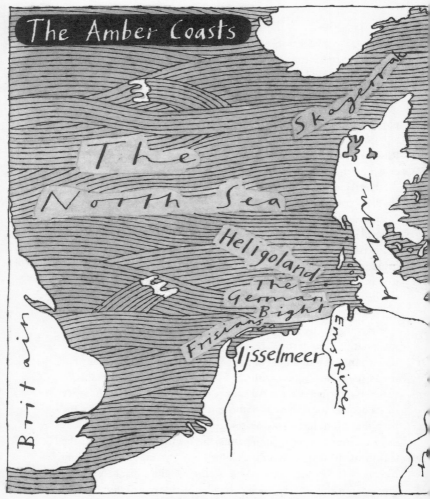

The Amber Coasts

Skagerak

Jutland

The North Sea

Heligoland

The German Bight

Frisians

Ijsselmeer

Ems River

Britain

Morava. It then skirted the eastern flank of the Alps, and passed through Slovenia, to the Gulf of Venice at the head of the Adriatic. It is easy to see, then, how in the distant past amber became associated with the Adriatic and with the Po valley, since it was here that it first became accessible to the Mediterranean community.

The alternative myths might also have within them some grains of reality. It is highly likely that some Jutish amber was transported

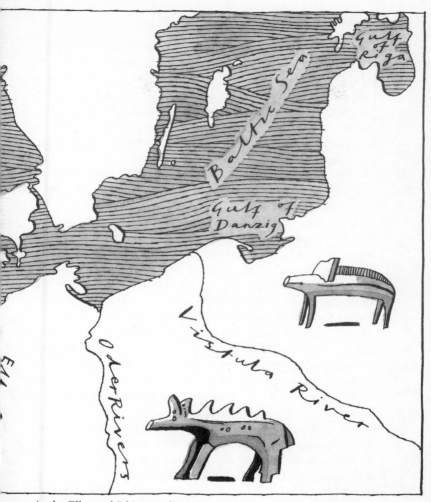

via the Elbe and Rhine to the Saône and thence down the Rhône, while some may have been brought to the Mediterranean from the Atlantic through Phoenician networks controlling the Pillars of Hercules. These alternative routes no doubt gave rise to the various myths that so enriched the Greek tradition.

It was all this fancy that the sober Herodotus was attempting to cut through in his politely dismissive remarks. Pliny the Elder was less tolerant. Before expounding in a rather exasperated way on the various myths surrounding amber he prepares his reader thus: 'Here is an opportunity for exposing the falsehoods of the Greeks. I only ask my readers to endure these with patience for it is important for mankind just to know that not all that the Greeks have recounted deserves to be admired' (*Nat. Hist.* 37.31). Pytheas would have known these fanciful stories and, as a scientist, will have shared Herodotus' caution. His northern journey would have given him the opportunity to explore the origins of amber for himself. Indeed it is tempting to believe that one of his prime aims may have been to research the source of amber, as well as that of tin.

Amber had been collected, exchanged and curated from the Neolithic period onwards, passing through intricate networks of exchange to reach most parts of Europe. By the first half of the second millennium BC the flow had grown to considerable proportions and sizeable pieces were finding their way into the burials of the Bronze Age élites extending from the Mycenaean world of Greece to the chalk plains of Wessex. In Greece at the tholos tombs of Kakovatos and in the shaft graves of Mycenae it is found as massive beads and perforated spacer plates to keep the strings of the beads apart, while in the barrow graves of Wessex gold-bound amber discs have been recovered as well as spectacular multi-strand necklaces, such as the fine example accompanying a woman's grave found at Upton Lovell in Wiltshire.

The most impressive of all of the British Bronze Age finds came from a barrow at Hove excavated in 1821. At the time the mound was 65 m. in diameter and 4 m. high and formed the focus of rural celebrations held every Good Friday, when hundreds of young people descended on it to play 'kiss-in-the-ring' and other games. Now it is no more, having been flattened to provide gardens for suburban Victorian villas. The excavation of 1821 exposed an oak coffin containing fragments of decayed bone, a stone axe-hammer, a bronze dagger, a whetstone and a handled cup cut from a single block of deep red amber which must originally have been at least 13 cm. across. It is a magnificent piece, rather like a round-bottomed teacup with a wide strap handle, decorated with incised grooves around the shoulder. Its wonderful translucence, lightness and rich colour must have made a profound impact on everyone who saw it. To consign such a rarity to the earth with the body of the chieftain required a supreme act of faith.

Once established in the Early Bronze Age, the 'trade' in amber continued unabated and over the years huge quantities flowed through the systems of exchange, much of it ending up in the graves of the élite. In a sixth-century BC burial found at Hochmichele, not far from the fortified residence of Heuneburg on the Danube, the grave goods accompanying one body included four amber rings and a necklace of 351 amber beads, while the rich female burial from Vix near Châtillon-sur-Seine wore a bracelet of twelve perforated cylindrical beads of amber strung on a copper alloy strip. One particularly intriguing item came from the burial at Grafenbühl near Asperg in southern Germany. Although the main grave chamber had been robbed a number of objects remained, including the bone carving of a sphinx with a face made of amber. The piece is clearly of Mediterranean workmanship and was probably made in Italy. The amber from which the face was fashioned must have been transported from the Baltic to Italy, where it was carved and attached to the sphinx before being exported northwards again to west-central Europe. This much-travelled piece of stone is a reminder of how complex the exchange networks could be.

The attractions of amber were many. Its rich variety of colour and its transparency make it a highly decorative substance. But there is more besides: it had a certain magical quality. Its lightness is a surprise and it also has electrostatic properties. This was remarked upon by the Venerable Bede, who noted that if it was 'warmed with rubbing', like jet, it 'holds fast whatever is applied to it'. Such a substance inevitably inspired awe and would have been a symbol of power and prestige in prehistoric Europe.

Pliny gives an indication of how it was considered in the Roman world. It was, he said, 'as yet fancied only by women'. There were several kinds:

The tawny is the more valuable: and still more so if it is transparent but the colour must not be too fiery: not a fiery glare but a mere suggestion of it is what we admire in amber. The most highly approved specimens are the 'Falernian', so called because they recall the colour of the wine: they are transparent and glow gently so as to have . . . the agreeably mellow tint of honey that has been reduced by boiling.   (*Nat. Hist.* 37.47)

He also mentions the least valuable types, the waxy and the pale kind, though the latter has the finest scent – a reminder that women liked to hold amber in their hands and smell it.

Like Bede, Pliny was interested in the electrostatic properties of the stone and attempted to explain them: 'When rubbing with the finger draws forth the hot exhalation, amber attracts straw, dry leaves and linden-bark, just as the magnet attracts iron.' The belief here is that the 'hot exhalation' displaced the air in front of the amber or magnet causing a vacuum which sucks in the lighter material or iron. This theory was developed by the seventeenth-century English physician William Gilbert, who, in his *De Magnete Magneticisque Corporibus*, published in 1600, first coined the word 'electricity', from *electrum*, the Greek name for amber.

By the first century AD it was well known that amber came from the shores of the North Sea and Pliny had a reasonably accurate appreciation of its nature:

amber is formed of a liquid seeping from the interior of a species of pine, just as the gum in a cherry-tree or the resin in a pine bursts forth when the liquid is excessively abundant. The exudation is hardened by frost or perhaps by moderate heat, or else the sea after a spring tide has carried off the pieces from the islands. At all events, the amber is washed up on the shores of the mainland, being swept along so easily that it seems to hover in the water without settling on the sea-bed.   (*Nat. Hist.* 11.42)

To Pliny's credible sketch we can now add more detail. The 'amber forests' grew in the Eocene period, between 40 and 50 million years ago, on the south edge of a land mass known as the Fennoscandian shield, incorporating the whole of present-day Scandinavia and

Finland. It was largely a temperate forest but warm enough in part to support more subtropical growth. Highly resinous trees like pine were common. Insects and parasitic plants, together with frequent violent storms, caused constant damage to the growing trees, encouraging the resin to flow. In normal aerobic conditions the resin would disintegrate along with the tangle of dead vegetation of which it was a part, but when the resin, consolidated as amber, was carried away by storms and flooding rivers into estuaries and was there quickly covered by other sediments, it was spared the rotting caused by aerobic conditions and became fossilized to become part of the Eocene formations. Millions of years later these sediments, now compacted by age and buried under huge weights of ice during the Ice Age, began to be elevated as the ice sheet melted. Rivers, cutting down through the old sediments, exposed the ancient deposits of amber, which were once more carried down to the sea. Because of their lightness the lumps of amber floated and were washed up, forming strand lines on beaches or deeper drifts in the more sheltered coves and inlets, rather as polythene bottles do today. Here the amber was to be had for the gathering. Elsewhere, exposed in the banks of the rivers, beds of amber could be quarried.

There are two principal sources of amber: Jutish amber, which occurs in a coastal band down the east coast of Jutland and Schleswig-Holstein along to the north coast of Holland, including the estuaries of the Elbe, Weser and Ems; and Baltic amber, found along the south Baltic coast, between the mouth of the Oder and the Gulf of Danzig, and also along the east Baltic coast from Kaliningrad to the Samland peninsula on the Gulf of Riga. In prehistoric times Jutish amber appears to have been the most extensively exploited, but by Roman times the Baltic amber had become an important resource. Pliny describes how, during the reign of Nero, a Roman knight was sent north from Carnuntum, a Roman fort on the Danube, via the Morava to the Baltic coast 370 km. away, to acquire a load of amber to decorate the fittings of the amphitheatre in Rome in preparation for a prestigious gladiatorial show. He excelled himself, bringing back huge quantities acquired in various markets, including one piece weighing 5 kg. So successful were his endeavours that even the nets protecting the podium from the wild bears were studded with amber.

By the early twentieth century Jutland was no longer a significant economic source while Samland was now providing 88 per cent of the world's supply.

A question which becomes particularly relevant to the discussion of Pytheas' exploration of the amber trade is which sources were being exploited in the fourth century BC. It is clear, from the richness of the Danish Bronze Age, that the communities of Jutland and the islands were able to acquire huge quantities of bronze through exchange with the bronze-producing area of the south. Since Denmark had no copper or tin of its own everything had to be imported in return for which Jutish amber is one of the most likely payments. Yet by the first century AD it was the southern and eastern Baltic deposits that were meeting Mediterranean demand. The period 700 BC–AD 100, therefore, saw the demise of the Jutish source and the rise of the Baltic. In all probability the change-over was gradual but by the fifth century BC the eastern amber route through Moravia and around the eastern side of the Alps was in operation and the élites of Slovenia who were able to command the route had ample supplies for their burials. Chemical analysis of the amber shows that the Etruscans were getting at least some of their amber from Baltic sources at this time. Taken together, the evidence would suggest that Pytheas' visit took place at just about the time that traditional supplies from Jutland were beginning to falter. Could this, perhaps, have been one of the things he wanted to assess for himself?

We last saw Pytheas resting on Orkney or Shetland thinking over the wonders he had seen in the far north. What then? One possibility is that he made his way southwards, along the east coast of Britain to Kantion, the south-eastern corner of Britain, having *en route* perhaps explored the Humber estuary and noted the chariot burial ritual practised by the inhabitants of the York Wolds and the York

Moors. At Kantion, or in the Thames estuary, he could have picked up stories about the amber coasts and islands to the east, before returning along the south coast of Britain, noting Vectis (the Isle of Wight), *en route* to Ushant to begin the last leg of his homeward journey. This is the minimalist explanation but is consistent with what little we know.

But there are two other alternatives. The less ambitious is that he travelled down the east coast of Britain to Kantion and there crossed to the Continent, working his way up the coast to Jutland to see the amber-producing region for himself. It is even possible that a shorter route was taken from East Anglia across the North Sea to the Netherlands. This would have required sailing along the latitude for a distance of about 120 nautical miles. A more demanding route is sometimes suggested, taking him direct from Orkney across the North Sea to the Skagerrak – the wide gulf between southern Norway and northern Jutland – to reach the east coast of Sweden somewhere in the region of present-day Göteborg. From here, it is argued, he sailed southwards into the Baltic to visit the amber coast around the mouth of the Oder.

There are, therefore, three possibilities for us to consider: that he learned of the amber coast only from informants, that he visited western Jutland or that he entered and explored the western Baltic.

Pytheas' reports on the amber-producing regions were used by Pliny in his *Natural Histories* but, surprisingly, not by Strabo. In the introduction to Book 4 Pliny summarizes what is to follow, mentioning, among other things, a discussion of the ninety-six islands of the 'Gallic Ocean' and listing Pytheas as one of his sources. In his fuller discussion later in the book he turns to the Northern Ocean, telling us that there are a large number of islands, many of them unnamed, in the region. One of them, called Baunonia, is

off Skythia by a day's voyage, where amber is cast up by waves in springtime – as Timaeus told . . . Xenophon of Lampsacus recounts that out from the Scythian shore by three days' voyage is an island of immense size, Balcia. Pytheas calls this 'Basilia'.   (*Nat. Hist.* 4.94–5)

Later, in Book 37, Pliny returns to a more detailed discussion of amber.

Pytheas [said] there is an estuary of the ocean occupied by the Guiones, a Germanic people, named Metuonis, 6,000 stades in extent. From here, the island Abalus is a day's voyage away, where [amber] is carried down by the floods in spring and excreted by the Congealed Sea; the local inhabitants use it as wood for fire and sell it to the neighbouring Teutoni. Timaeus also believed [Pytheas] but called the island Basilia.   (Nat. Hist. 37.35–6)

There is some evident confusion here but some of the same material, presumably derived from Pytheas but without acknowledgement, is repeated by Diodorus Siculus:

There is an island in the open sea towards the Ocean right opposite Skythia which is above Galatia, referred to by the name Basileia. On to it the sea throws up a quantity of what is called amber [which] appears nowhere else in the inhabited world ... The amber is collected on the ... island and taken by the locals to the mainland through which it is carried to places in our region. (5.23.1)

As is so often the case, the geography is confused by the use of different terminologies. At the time when Pytheas was writing it was believed that Europe was occupied by two different barbarian peoples – the Celts in the west and the Scythians in the east. Thus it followed that if one sailed north-eastwards along the Northern Ocean coast of Europe one would pass from the lands of the Celts to the lands of the Scyths. Diodorus adds a further refinement, introducing Galatia between Keltikē and the land of the Skyths. Through Galatia, he said, passed the rivers Rhine, Rhône and Danube. Clearly this geography is difficult, but the association of Galatia with the Rhine indicates that he was probably vaguely referring to what is now Belgium and Holland.

Pliny uses the old cognitive geography of 'the Skythian coast' in his Book 4 but in Book 37 writes about the Germans occupying this area. The concept of a distinct ethnic race of Germans living largely north of the Rhine was popularized by the *Commentaries* of Julius Caesar and by the later campaigns of Augustus and Tiberius which had thoroughly penetrated the region as far east as the Elbe. Although Pliny would have had much up-to-date material to work on it is curious that he did not bother to modify the archaic geography used by his sources in Book 4. It may simply be that he had little interest in these dull northern coastal regions. They were, as Tacitus records at the end of the first century AD, seldom navigated by Mediterranean shipping. No one really wanted to go there 'where nature offers nothing but scenes of deformity, where the inclemency of the seasons never relents; where the land presents a dreary prospect without form or culture'.

The principal features in Pytheas' description are a wide estuary called Metuonis and an offshore island variously named. The word which Pliny uses for estuary – *aestuarium* – is usually used in the context of a river mouth or delta area – a tidal zone of shoals and mud flats, exposed at low tide, giving way to marshland above the tidal limit. It is a region where fresh water mixes with sea water and where the line between sea and land is indistinct and variable, the one merging into the other. The difficulty with Pliny's description is the size of the 'estuary' – 6,000 stades, or 1,100 km. This is colossal for a single estuary and some have argued that it can only be accepted if it is assumed that Pytheas was in some way referring to the western end of the Baltic. Alternatively the figure may be in error, either the result of a mistake in transmission or an over-estimate resulting from Pytheas misjudging the distance travelled by sea in a day. If this second option is preferred the 'estuary' would still have to be large, certainly not much less than 800 km.

Where then is the estuarine zone of Metuonis? The simplest solution would be to suppose that it included the entire North Sea coast from the vicinity of Dunkirk to the tip of Jutland, encompassing the mouths of the Meuse, Rhine, Ems, Weser and Elbe. At its maximum extremities this fugitive coast, with its sand and gravel bars, its great area of marshland and its wide estuaries, is about 1,200 km. in length. The innermost part, from the Ijsselmeer, near Amsterdam, to Jammerbugt at the north of Jutland, is about

700 km. long. It flanks the south and east sides of the German Bight, incorporating the estuaries of the Ems, Weser and Elbe and thus includes the whole of the amber coast of northern Holland, Schleswig-Holstein and Jutland. At whatever point Pytheas or his informants crossed to the Continent – the narrow crossing from Kent to near Dunkirk or the longer crossing from East Anglia to Ijsselmeer – the coastwise journey to the tip of Jutland would have seemed like a huge unending estuary fed by a multiplicity of rivers which the sea was ever trying to block by building barriers of sand and gravel across their mouths. It was hardly an inviting landscape.

Somewhere off the coast was an island or islands where amber was to be had. Here there is further confusion in the texts. Pliny gives three conflicting accounts: it was called *Baunonia* by Timaeus and lay one day's sail from the mainland; it was called *Balcia* by Xenophon (but *Basilia* by Pytheas) and lay three days away; it was called *Abalus* by Pytheas (*Basilia* by Timaeus) and was one day from the mainland. Diodorus' account is much the same but provides the alternative spelling *Basileia*. The simplest way to explain the apparent muddle is to suppose that Pliny made an error in saying that the Balcia of Xenophon was called Basilia by Timaeus. One ingenious classical scholar offered a suggestion of how this could have come about, arguing that the Latin text should have read *Pytheas Abalum, Timaeus Basiliam*: 'Abalus by Pytheas, Basilia by Timaeus', and that the two middle words were at some stage omitted. Although this might appear to be a piece of over-elaborate special pleading it neatly resolves the problem, while at the same time providing a timely warning that classical texts may not be all they seem.

If we allow the emendation then the amber island was known as Abalus by Pytheas but was also called Basilia/Balcia/Basileia and possibly Baunonia. The name Abalus may come from the Celtic word *aball* – 'apple' – though why the island was so named is obscure. The second name is almost certainly the Greek adjective *basileia*, meaning 'royal'. This might explain why the island could have two names – the Celtic name by which it was known locally and a descriptive name applied to it by the Greeks, reflecting what they perceived to be its status: it was an island ruled by a king.

There is little that can usefully be said about the Guiones who Pytheas tells us lived in the region or about their neighbours the Teutones, except that both were known to have occupied parts of what is now the Jutland peninsula.

The exact location of Abalus/Basilia has been a popular subject for debate. Of immense size and three days out from the mainland, says Xenophon, while the others are non-committal on its size but agree on its being one day's sailing away. Heligoland, 50 km. from the mainland, would be about right for distance but it is hardly of immense size. The island is admirably sited in relation to the difficult shores of the Netherlands and Jutland, being well clear of the long but fragmented coastal barriers represented now by the string of offshore islands – the West and East Frisian Islands, guarding the northern coast of the Netherlands and Germany, and the North Frisian Islands, which stretch along the east coast of Jutland. Anyone entering the German Bight and making for the estuaries of the Weser or Elbe would use Heligoland as a point of reference. The island is hardly impressive – only about a kilometre in extent – but its red cliffs, 60 m. high, create a reassuring and easily recognizable landmark on an otherwise difficult approach. Such a place would have made an ideal offshore port-of-trade.

Pliny and Diodorus do not have much to say of the local inhabitants except that they placed little value on their amber because they burned it. This is a curious observation. It would be necessary to consume huge quantities to provide sufficient heat to roast a pig or warm a house. A more likely explanation is that the burning was a ritual practice, perhaps a propitiatory act concerned with returning the amber to the deities who controlled the sky. The association of amber with the sun in Greek mythology would go some way to support this.

Other than this tiny scrap of observation, and the names which Pliny records, the people are anonymous, but archaeology has done much to fill the void. The heaths and marshlands of the region provide excellent conditions for the preservation of settlement evidence and the archaeologists of the region have done much to exploit the potential. What emerges is a picture suggesting a considerable similarity in settlement type over the whole region from the Rhine/Meuse estuary to the tip of Jutland, and an impression of social and economic stability over much of the first millennium BC and well into the first millennium AD.

One of the most extensively excavated settlements is Grøntoft in west Jutland where the entire history of a village has been traced from its foundation about 500 BC to its final abandonment some time in the third century BC. Over the three hundred years or so of its life the site of the village wandered about a restricted landscape with each rebuilding. Normally there were about twelve individual farmhouses in use at any one time, all clustered together within a fenced outer enclosure, but the frequent rebuildings meant that the archaeologists had to deal with about two hundred and fifty individual houses overall. The typical farmhouse was a long rectangular structure 5–6 m. wide and up to 20 m. long. The roof was supported on two rows of aisle posts while the walls were of vertical timbers or wattle-and-daub. The usual plan was to divide the house into two halves by means of a cross passage. One half was the family living-space, while the other half was divided into separate stalls for cattle. At one stage, in the third century BC, when the village was made up of twelve houses, five of them had provision for 8–18 cattle, two were smaller, with only 3 or 4 cows, while three of the houses had no provision for animals at all. An analysis of all the evidence from this phase of the village suggests that there were 8–10 families – some fifty individuals – having 70–80 head of cattle. Life appears to have been led at a simple but stable level. The surrounding fields provided wheat and barley as staples while the cattle ensured a constant supply of milk and cheese. When eventually they were slaughtered there was meat to be had, their hides possibly providing a small surplus for local trade.

Much of this long coastal region was marshland which was flooded from time to time as the relative sea-level fluctuated. In periods of lower sea-level farms were established on drier areas to exploit the rich grazing round about. In the Ems estuary archaeologists have found farming settlements every two or three km. alongside the river. A typical example at Boomborg-Hatzum consisted of six three-aisled farmhouses, together with their outhouses and granaries, clustered around a central open area. The settlement had been built directly on the surface of the marsh but had to be abandoned in the third century BC, as the land flooded in a period of higher sea-level, driving the population inland to the drier, but less fertile, sandy soils.

Although there was a degree of instability caused by fluctuating sea-levels along the coastal fringes, overall the picture which emerges is of economic and social stability based on a well-established mixed farming regime. What stands out is the apparent lack of significant wealth differentiation. In each village there would probably have been a head man but there is little evidence of there ever having been powerful élites or the need to display prowess in the form of elaborate buildings. This was in marked contrast to contemporary societies in Britain.

Would Pytheas have been aware of all this? Possibly not. Given the difficulty of the coastline and the general inaccessibility of the mainland from the sea, it is quite probable that traders went no further than the island of Abalus/Basilia to which the amber was brought. Abalus then was to amber what Ictis was to tin. We can imagine the communities of the amber coast collecting amber from the exposures in river banks and the shores in the slack periods in the farming cycle and exchanging it for the few external luxuries that they needed. Some ended up on Abalus for the maritime traders to collect, some was exchanged with neighbours and found its way into the networks reaching southern Europe by way of the great rivers. Traders from Britain would have no need to go further than the island: the marshy mainland beyond remained a *terra incognita*.

Pytheas could, of course, have learned about the amber island from the comfort of a British east coast port. He makes no claim to have seen it for himself, but would such a man have been content with that when all he had to do was to join a local ship on its trading venture? We can imagine him setting out, perhaps from

Kantion, quickly crossing the stretch of open sea to the Belgian coast and then making the long haul of some 500 km. north-eastwards, keeping the coast of the Netherlands and the long chain of Frisian Islands comfortably in sight, to arrive at Abalus, most likely Heligoland, four or five days later.

He had now discovered the sources of tin and amber as well as reaching the limits of the cosmos. His exploration of the Atlantic was complete: it was time to make for home.

The return journey would probably have taken him along the south coast of Britain, noting the Isle of Wight, *en route* to his starting-point in Belerion, thus completing the circumnavigation of the island. From here it was the familiar way back to Armorica. Taking this route it is easy to see why Pytheas would have claimed, as Strabo records, 'that Kantion is some days sail of Keltikē'.

From Armorica Pytheas could have been back home in Massalia within a month.

RETURN TO OBLIVION

The last leg of the homeward journey from Narbo to Massalia would have been a time for contemplation. A familiar Greek merchant ship sailing the placid Mediterranean would have provided a welcome contrast to the bizarre craft of the Atlantic and unpredictable wildness of the Ocean: it would have been a reminder that life was fast returning to normal. Knowing so little of Pytheas the man we cannot begin to guess how he felt as the ship approached Massalia. Was he the fearless traveller returning from the unknown, eager for the clamorous attention of the crowd and the heaped rewards of the civic authorities, or a more humble scholar satisfied at having probed the edges of the world but fearful of how his contemporaries might react to his stories of remote lands and alien peoples? Was his homecoming heralded or did he arrive unnoticed? These things we shall never know. Nor can we guess what he might have brought back with him – sacks of amber and tin ingots and bales of furs or a small lump of amber to hold in his hand reminding him of the Great Estuary, and a knuckle-bone of tin to put on his desk as a memento of the friendly traders of Belerion. What we do know is that he brought back knowledge – precise observations carefully recorded and an entirely new understanding of the world.

Much of what he had discovered would have been of direct use to the entrepreneurs of his city. By the end of the fourth century a new world order was beginning to grip the Mediterranean as Rome emerged as a dominant force, requiring its rapid growth to be fuelled with ever-increasing supplies of raw material and manpower. The extension of Roman power throughout the Italian peninsula provided some new markets and new resources, but Rome's economy needed the broader arena of the western Mediterranean in which to expand and its friendly relations with Massalia and the other Greek cities of the Golfe du Lion became of increasing importance. Commercial relationships between the two cities, bound by the treaty drawn up in 390 BC, flourished. Massalia was, among other things, the port-of-trade through which commodities of all kinds passed. As the demands of the Mediterranean grew so the imperative to develop overland trade with the interior took hold. By thoroughly exploring the Aude–Garonne route and the sea lanes beyond to the very source of the tin Pytheas had demystified the system, opening it up for others to develop further and to regularize. Thereafter the corridor to the Atlantic played an increasingly important part in the western Mediterranean economy.

While there must surely have been a commercial motive behind his expedition, Pytheas was first and foremost a scientist drawn to the edges of the world in search of firm answers to the uncertainties and doubts raised by earlier writers such as the cautious Herodotus. Insofar as we can judge the nature of his book *On the Ocean* it was a sober account of a wide range of data collected first-hand. As such it belongs to the style of work being produced by such men as Eudoxus of Cnidos, Heraclides of Pontus and Aristotle around the middle of the fourth century, rather than to the slightly later style of more theoretical writing appearing in the last decades of the century. This has led some scholars to suggest that his journey may have taken place about 350, but against this is the argument that *On the Ocean* was not quoted by Aristotle, writing in the period 335–323, and that had he known of Pytheas' work he would certainly have made use of it. While it is, of course, possible that the book did not circulate widely at first, and may simply have been unknown in the eastern Mediterranean in Aristotle's lifetime, the novelty of the information that Pytheas brought back and the extensive maritime links that bound the entire Mediterranean make it difficult to believe that it would have taken much time for knowledge of the work to reach Athens. The first person to quote Pytheas was a pupil of Aristotle, Dicaearchus, who was active in the period 326–296. On balance, then, it is reasonable to assume that *On the Ocean* did not become widely known until about 320, although we must allow that it may have been written a little before, and it may have taken a while for Pytheas to commit his new-found knowledge to writing.

What manner of book was *On the Ocean*? To judge from the surviving fragments it was a general scientific work with sections devoted to astronomy, the ocean, and the geography of north-west Atlantic Europe. This much is reasonably clear but how the book was structured it is difficult to say. One tantalizing clue comes in a very roundabout way from a work of the fourth century AD attributed to an unknown writer referred to as the Scholiast to Apollonius. He was a grammarian who wrote a general guide to the commentaries that had been compiled in the first and second centuries AD to a poem, *Argonautika*, written in the second century BC by Apollonius of Rhodes. Apollonius in turn gleaned some of his information from Pytheas, probably indirectly through another source. The scrap we have therefore comes to us fifth-hand, having been passed on over the course of seven centuries. Little wonder that it is slightly muddled! What the Scholiast gives is a brief mention of the volcanic Aeolian Islands to the north of Sicily, adding: 'These things Pytheas recounts in *Circuit of the Earth* saying also that the sea boils.'

Here is fertile ground indeed for speculation. But first the title of the book. *Circuit of the Earth* was a common title used for books in the fourth century BC and is probably best explained simply as an error for *On the Ocean* rather than implying that Pytheas wrote two separate books. The fact that he appears to have written about underwater volcanic activity around the Aeolian Islands at first seems odd, but one plausible suggestion is that in *On the Ocean*, when describing the nature of the sea, he contrasted the freezing sea of the north with the boiling sea in the Mediterranean. In other words he was placing his northern observations in a broader and more theoretical context, pointing up the differences by contrasting them to the more familiar world. The speculation, sometimes made, that he was writing about the volcanoes of Iceland or the hot springs of Britain, is unnecessarily far-fetched.

On the Ocean was well known to two of Pytheas' near contemporaries, Dicaearchus of Messene and Timaeus of Tauromenium. Dicaearchus was a geographer with a special interest in astronomy, while Timaeus was a historian whose principal work was a history of his native Sicily. Timaeus was the son of the tyrant (ruler) of Tauromenium, a major city on the east coast of Sicily, but was exiled from the island by Agathocles, the rival tyrant of Syracuse, and went to live in Athens. The precise dates of his exile are not known but it is generally believed that he left Sicily about 330 and was active in Athens until about 280. He would therefore have been an exact contemporary of Dicaearchus, who was operating between 326 and 296: it is inconceivable that the two scholars did not know each other. The Athenian élite was comparatively small and there would have been ample opportunity for them to meet to debate issues of mutual interest and exchange information. One particularly intriguing possibility is that Timaeus, who would most probably have maintained his links with Sicily and with all the information sources of the west Mediterranean, might have been responsible for introducing Pytheas' book to Athens. In any event both men made use of it in their own work.

Dicaearchus wrote a major geographical work, *Circuit of the Earth*, in which, assuming the world to be a sphere, he attempted to map the known world, using a central parallel running through Rhodes. The inhabitable world, he believed, ran from just south of Meroe on the Nile almost to the Arctic Circle, a distance of 40,000 stades. In allowing that people lived so far north he was breaking with received wisdom and in this may well have been relying on Pytheas, although Strabo says that 'not even Dicaearchus' accepted his accounts of the northern regions. Even so it is probable that Dicaearchus used Pytheas' sun heights in establishing his latitudes. Nothing survives of *Circuit of the Earth* so we have to rely entirely on brief references in the works of other writers.

The same is true of Timaeus' *History*, although the book survived long enough for Cicero to enjoy and Pliny to quote from. As a Greek from Sicily Timaeus was concerned to emphasize the achievements of the western Greeks to counterbalance the Athenian bias of many contemporary works. For this reason, he was keen to praise men like Pytheas and to proclaim their achievements. Pliny used Timaeus as a source for information about Britain and the amber-producing regions of the North Sea for his *Natural History* and it is likely that a later Sicilian writer, Diodorus, also used him, although, unlike Pliny, he does not acknowledge his source.

By the end of the first quarter of the third century *On the Ocean* was beginning to be known throughout the Mediterranean and was already being used as a source of astronomical and anthropological information. In physical form the text of *On the Ocean* would have been written on a papyrus roll about 20 cm. wide wound between wooden batons, and copies would have been made by scribes whenever they were required (with all the opportunity that gave of introducing error). We know comparatively little of the early book trade but scraps gleaned from Greek texts throw some light on the matter. The comic poet Eupolis, writing in the fifth century, tells us that one corner of the Athenian agora was set aside for the sale of books, which implies that enterprising scribes made a livelihood copying best-sellers. Authors, too, had copies of their works made to be given to their friends. It may have been in this way that *On the Ocean* first went into circulation. One can imagine Pytheas having copies of his book made in Massalia for his supporters and those interested in following up his remarkable discoveries. Eventually one of the copies could have reached a Greek port in Sicily where a friend of Timaeus might have spotted it and had a copy made and sent on to him. By some such progression *On the Ocean* reached Athens by about 300 BC.

Once in circulation in the city a text as novel and surprising as this would have become widely known and such men as Dicaearchus and Timaeus would have made notes for use in their own works. Just such a process is described by Socrates (quoted by the historian Xenophon): 'Together with my friends I unroll and go through the treasures which the wise men of old bequeathed to us in their books and if we come across anything good we excerpt it.' Scholars were also quite ready to 'edit' earlier texts. Plutarch tells the story of the young Alcibiades, who, anxious to acquire a copy of Homer, accosted a succession of schoolmasters, one of whom told him he did indeed have a copy, which he had corrected himself. The ownership of books, at least among the educated classes, seems to have been quite widespread in Athens. Aristophanes in his play *Frogs* claims, rather sweepingly perhaps, that 'everyone has a book' and later goes on to poke fun at Euripides for the large library he had accumulated. Some personal libraries were quite specialist, such as the collection of works of the famous Sophists brought together by a young scholar, Euthydemus. But the best-known library of its day was that established by Aristotle at the Lyceum in Athens. It became the model for the world-famous libraries established by the Hellenistic rulers who came to power following the break-up of Alexander's empire at the end of the fourth century – roughly coincident with Pytheas' voyage.

The greatest of these libraries was established at Alexandria by Ptolemy I about 295, as an adjunct to the Museum. The Museum should not be thought of in its popular present-day sense, as essentially a repository of artefacts, but as a place where scholars could commune with the Muses who presided over all the arts – in other words it was a research centre where a small group of scholars could indulge their skills supported by the state, and since the Ptolemaic rulers were cultivated men, the support was ample and assured. It was not surprising therefore that one observer called them 'fattened fowls that quarrel without end in the hen-coop of the Museum'.

The Museum and Library of Alexandria were based on the model of Plato's Academy and Aristotle's Lyceum at Athens. Indeed, it was one of Aristotle's pupils, Demetrius of Phaleron, who advised Ptolemy I in setting them up. The Library very soon became the largest in the world. Estimates of its size varied but a reasonable estimate would be about half a million volumes. Something of its size can be appreciated when it is known that the Library catalogue ran to 120 volumes.

To create such a collection the Ptolemies sent agents all over the Greek world to buy manuscripts. Ptolemy III added a major collection of works by the playwrights Aeschylus, Sophocles and Euripides, while his immediate successor concentrated on Homer. Ptolemy III was advised by a Chief Librarian, Eratosthenes. Eratosthenes was a creative scholar in his own right who in the middle of the third century produced a major work on geography in which he relied heavily on observations made by Pytheas. It is a reasonable assumption that *On the Ocean* was by this time on the Library shelves. The particular value of the great Alexandrian collection was its comprehensiveness and the fact that it contained many different editions of the same texts, facilitating the work of scholars in collecting and editing the classic texts and providing all those who had freedom to use the collection with the opportunity of gleaning observations and facts for their own scientific works from the near totality of recorded knowledge.

Slightly later on the scene came the Library established by the Attalid dynasty at their capital, Pergamum, in what is now western Turkey. The Library was begun by Attalus I in the last decades of the third century and continued by his son Eumenes. Once more the models used were the Academy and Lyceum at Athens and, while not rivalling Alexandria, the collection was said to have had 200,000 volumes. The Library occupies a dramatic position almost on the crest of a great hill, with the rest of the town cascading down the slopes below. It was appropriately sited close to the temple of Athena, goddess of learning. The whole area has been excavated and five rooms of the Library are now exposed, one of which is sufficiently well preserved to show the holes in the walls for the brackets to support the book-shelves. Together these rooms could have held about 17,000 volumes, so either the figure given by the classical sources is a gross overestimate or other Library buildings have still to be identified.

The Attalids were manic book-collectors. Their desire to acquire the unique library of Aristotle, at this time at Scepsis in north-west Asia Minor, forced the owners to hide it underground where damp and decay took their toll, damaging some of the precious texts beyond recovery. Their insatiable appetite for books is said to have provided forgers with a ready market.

Inevitably the two libraries became rivals. Matters came to a head when, to hinder the Pergamenes, Ptolemy V cut off the export of papyrus, and since Egypt was virtually the only source of supply this caused serious problems for Pergamum. But not to be outdone, Eumenes II turned to a traditional method used for centuries by the Ionian Greeks – instead of papyrus cured sheepskins were used. This new-style 'Pergamene paper' gives us the word parchment. Apart from expense, the principal disadvantage of using skins was that the skins were thicker and could not be easily used in roll form. Instead they were sewn together along one edge to create a paged book or codex. Books of this kind were, of course, much easier to read and to refer to than the cumbersome papyrus rolls and the innovation soon began to catch on.

The kingdom of Pergamum passed into Roman control at the end of the second century but the Great Library survived for another hundred years until Mark Antony decided to ship the entire collection to Alexandria as a gift to the last of the Ptolemaic rulers, Cleopatra. The transfer of the books would have gone some way to compensate for losses sustained a few years earlier when, during the conflict between Caesar and Pompey, a fire destroyed part of the collection. From an early date the Great Library was supplemented by a daughter collection associated with the temple of Serapis. Early in the 270s AD the Great Library was probably destroyed when the Palace Quarter in which it was situated was devastated, but the daughter library at the Serapeum continued for another century until it too was destroyed in 391.

How the few papyrus scrolls bearing the story of Pytheas' journey fared during the six centuries or so from the time *On the Ocean* was first written around 320 BC and the destruction of the Great Library *c.* AD 270 it is impossible to say though it is quite likely that at least one copy remained available to scholars at Alexandria throughout this period. Another copy would probably have been available at

Pergamum until the Library was trans-shipped and others may have survived in smaller libraries at Athens, Rhodes, Antioch and elsewhere. Most of the later scholars who consulted *On the Ocean* first-hand would, however, have done so at Alexandria.

One of the first seems to have been Eratosthenes of Cyrene, one of the greatest scholars of antiquity, who wrote on virtually every aspect of knowledge – grammar, philosophy, history, geography, geometry and astronomy – from his privileged position as Chief Librarian of the Great Library. He was born about 275 BC at Cyrene, a Greek city founded on the coast of what is now Libya, and studied in Athens before going to Alexandria as tutor to Ptolemy's son. He became Chief Librarian of the Great Library and died about 196 BC of voluntary starvation, having gone blind and lost the will to live. Nothing of his prodigious output survives save by reference or quotation in the works of others. His contemporaries thought he spread himself too wide to be a first-rank scholar (hence his nickname 'Beta') but as a geographer he made major contributions to knowledge.

His best-known work, the *Geography* produced in three books, was extensively referred to by Strabo. It must have been a seminal study far in advance of its time. His estimate of the circumference of the world is remarkably accurate, being between only 1 and 12 per cent out, depending on which stade measure he used. He also estimated that the known world, when measured E–W, extended for a little more than a third of the circumference of the globe on the Gibraltar–Ganges line. He was not far wrong: the actual measurement is 130° of the 360°. His other innovation was to begin to establish some of the latitudes running through Europe. Altogether his *Geography* was a stunning achievement.

It is interesting to find such a man accepting information recorded by Pytheas. In six separate passages Strabo refers to Eratosthenes' use of Pytheas, quoting him on such subjects as the location of Thule, Britannikē, the westerly extent of the Armorican peninsula and Iberia. It would seem that Eratosthenes was quite prepared to accept Pytheas' description of the remote north-west as an objective account of what no Greek had seen before.

The geographical work of Eratosthenes was widely known and formed the basis upon which Hipparchus developed his mathematical system of parallels. Hipparchus was born at Nicaea in Bithynia (north-western Turkey). He spent time at Alexandria but for most of his creative years he lived and worked in Rhodes. His precise dates are not recorded but he is known to have been active between about 160 and 130 BC. Hipparchus was more a mathematical astronomer than a geographer and was therefore more interested in Pytheas' sun height measurements and observations of the stars than his tales of the ocean coasts and their strange inhabitants. His one surviving book, *Commentary on the 'Phenomena' of Aratos and Eudoxos*, mentions, with approval, Pytheas' observations of star positions around the point of true north while in another book, *Against Eratosthenes* – a critique of his predecessor's views, known only from Strabo's discussion of it – he was evidently well content to accept Pytheas' measurements of sun heights at the solstice, which he converted into parallels of latitude.

That three of the greatest scientists of the third and second centuries and one of the foremost historians were ready to use *On the Ocean* without any apparent reservations says much for the standing of Pytheas in the eyes of his near contemporaries.

But not all were prepared to accept the veracity of Pytheas' work. The historian Polybius, who worked at about the same time as Hipparchus, was vitriolic in his contempt. To understand why, it is necessary to say something of Polybius the man and the complex agendas, both personal and political, he was working to.

Polybius was a Greek born about 200 BC into the ranks of the élite in the city of Megalopolis. He grew up there as a privileged member of the nobility, at the time when Rome was growing daily in strength and ambition, but when Achaea (Greece) was still free. But this was not to last. In 168 BC at the battle of Pydna the Roman armies, led by Aemilius Paullus, overcame Greek resistance and thus began the long period of Roman domination. In the aftermath of the battle Achaea was plundered of its artworks and a thousand political prisoners, one of them Polybius, were transported to Rome. For Polybius, now in his early thirties, it was an exciting opportunity not least because he soon befriended Paullus' son Scipio Aemilianus and was able to live with the family throughout his stay, enjoying all the benefits of their powerful patronage.

It was in Rome that he conceived of the idea of writing a *History*. It was aimed at an Achaean readership and set out to explain the Roman constitution and why Rome had become the dominant power in the Mediterranean. He is quite explicit about this. 'Who', he asks, 'is so thoughtless and so irresponsible as not to wish to know by what means, and under what kind of constitution, the Romans succeeded in subjecting nearly the whole inhabited world to their sole rule in not quite fifty-three years – an event unique in history?' As first conceived, the *Histories* were to cover the period from 220 to 168 but he was later to extend it to 146. The final work was published in forty books. Books 1–33 took the story up to 153. Book 34 was devoted to geography while the remainder, 35–40, covered the period 152–146.

The work of writing and editing occupied him for about fifty years – the latest details being added after 118 – although parts of the work would have been published much earlier when complete: the first fifteen books covering 168–150 were probably issued by 147 and most of those would have been written while he was in Rome.

His exile, and that of his surviving contemporaries, ended in 150 when the Roman Senate agreed to send the remaining three hundred back home. Many were now quite old, prompting Cato to joke about handing them over to the tender mercies of the Greek undertakers. Polybius would have been about 50. By this time he had acquired a taste for travel. A year or so before he had joined the entourage of his friend Scipio, whose office required him to visit North Africa and Spain, and a little later he explored the route which Hannibal had taken across the Alps. He had just reached home, in 149, when he was invited to join the Romans, as an adviser, in their new campaign against Carthage. He relished the opportunity and in 146, in the company of his friend Scipio, he witnessed the Romans' savage destruction of the great city. A few months later, using a ship supplied by Scipio, he sailed through the

Pillars of Hercules and into the Atlantic, travelling south down the coast of Africa and north along the west coast of Iberia. His new-found knowledge, gained, as he tells us, in 'journeys through Africa, Spain and Gaul, and voyages on the seas that lie on the farther side of these countries', excited him: he now saw himself as the interpreter of the remote west for his eastern Greek audience.

He returned home to Megalopolis not long after the Roman destruction of Corinth in the autumn of 146. In the years that followed there would have been trips to Rome and it is even possible that he joined Scipio during the Roman siege of the Celtiberian city of Numantia in northern Iberia in 133, but for the most part Polybius probably remained in his native city until his death, soon after 118, at the age of 82, caused, we are told, by a fall from his horse. One highly significant journey, made sometime during the reign of Ptolemy Euergetes II, probably soon after 145, was to Alexandria. Here, it is not unreasonable to suppose, he spent time researching for his *Histories* in the Great Library. The potential significance of this to our story we shall return to in a moment.

Polybius was a highly competent historian writing about events largely within his own lifetime. From his privileged position as an Achaean aristocrat, and later a close confidant of Scipio, he was intimately involved with the powerful men of his day and, as we have seen, was actually present at many of the deciding moments of history. Access and experience ensured that his *Histories* had a crisp accuracy. Yet he was not without personal foibles which affected his judgement and led him into tirades of polemic. As a man of action involved in the making of history he had no time for armchair historians. 'It will be well with history', he wrote, 'either when men of action undertake to write it ... or again when would-be historians regard a training in practical affairs as essential to their craft.' Here he was echoing Plato but it is a neat example of writing the job description to suit oneself! The principal recipient of this particular attack was Timaeus – a man who admitted that he was ignorant of warfare and the real world but who believed that by spending nearly fifty years in the libraries of Athens he had all the materials he needed to write history. Polybius had a point and was right in his criticisms of some of Timaeus' judgments, but his attack was surely more personally motivated. Timaeus was, as Polybius was forced to admit, a competent and thorough historian, although he could not resist adding that 'in certain matters I know of no author of repute who seems to have been more inexperienced and more careless'. Still, Timaeus was a good historian with an international reputation: by demeaning him Polybius could hope to build his own reputation on his rival's shoulders – a not unknown procedure in the academic world.

There may, however, have been another irritation. Polybius visited Alexandria sometime between 145 and 135. Could it have been, as one French scholar has recently argued, that on this visit Polybius came to realize that Timaeus was widely regarded as the principal authority on the remote regions of the west – an expertise that Polybius, by virtue of his recent travels, wanted to claim as his own? It is an interesting hypothesis and can be taken still further. Perhaps it was on his visit to Alexandria that Polybius saw for the first time a copy of Pytheas' *On the Ocean* and suddenly realized that his own exploration of the Atlantic in 146 had been dramatically upstaged by Pytheas more than a century and a half earlier. His venomous attack on Pytheas' veracity has all the hallmarks of intense academic jealousy.

At some stage in the writing of the *Histories*, after his Atlantic voyage in 146, Polybius made additions to the text of his already published Book 3, saying that at a later stage in the work he will write about the barbarians of Iberia who live between the Mediterranean and the Atlantic and that he will give an account of the Pillars of Hercules, the Outer Ocean, the British Isles and the tin trade and the gold and silver mines of Iberia, based on his own travels in Africa, Spain, Gaul and on the Atlantic. In stating the intention he was referring to Book 34, devoted to geography, which he had just written or was about to write. Sadly, very little of the book survives in its original form, although something of its content can be reconstructed from quotations in the works of Strabo, Athenaeus and Pliny the Elder.

As far as can be judged, the book was composed of a general

description of the world, a more detailed description of Europe and a *periegesis* of Africa. It was to provide a background to the historical narrative but the real *raison d'être* was to present Polybius' own observations of Iberia, Gaul, Africa and the more remote regions of the Atlantic as significant and original contributions to knowledge. To do this he had to dismiss all previous claims. Against this background one can understand his particular irritation with Pytheas and also with Timaeus, whose widely read work quoted Pytheas, apparently quite extensively and with approval. He could deal with Timaeus by saying that in 'certain matters' he was careless and inexperienced but Pytheas he had personally to discredit in a deliberate act of character assassination. This he did by contrasting himself – an aristocrat whose powerful friend, the famous Scipio Aemilianus, had provided him with resources to travel – with Pytheas, 'a private individual and a poor man at that'. How could such a person cover the great distance he claimed to have travelled 'by ship and by foot'. Worse still, was the implication, he was a merchant and such men could not be trusted: they would tell you 'false and sensational stories'. All Pytheas' claims were bogus, although 'many people have been led astray by [him]'. Among those, he implies, who were 'led astray' were Timaeus, Eratosthenes and Dicaearchus, each of whom, in turn, comes in for criticism.

Polybius' attack on the reputation of Pytheas was thorough and effective. Whether or not he quoted evidence in Book 34 to try to disprove Pytheas or simply relied on invective and innuendo as would appear to be the case from Strabo's quotations, we cannot be sure, but once made the accusation stuck.

The attack on Pytheas' credibility was driven home still further by Strabo, who wrote at the end of the first century BC and early in the first century AD. Strabo was born sometime around 64–63 BC at Amaseia, the capital of the kingdom of Pontus, which occupied the north-eastern part of Asia Minor (now Turkey) stretching along the south shore of the Black Sea. His birth coincided with the conquest of the area by Pompey and he would have grown up, a member of the native élite, at the time when

Pontus was being absorbed into the Roman empire. He was taught Greek by the best available teachers and went on to complete his education in Rome during a five-year stay in his early twenties. At some stage in his early years he served in the Roman administration in his home region and travelled quite widely around the eastern Mediterranean area, spending some time at Alexandria. Eventually, in 29 BC, at the age of about 33, he settled in Rome, there to spend the rest of his life writing his *Historical Memoranda* in 47 books and an accompanying *Geography* in 17 books. He died about AD 24 at the age of about 80. Such was his largely unremarkable life.

Historical Memoranda probably covered the period from the destruction of Carthage in 146 (where Polybius' *Histories* left off) to the fall of Alexandria to the Romans in 31 BC. The work was never widely known and had disappeared totally by the early second century AD. *Geography* on the other hand seems to have been completely unknown until about AD 100, or if it was known it was not quoted by any of the first-century writers whose works survive. Thereafter it was quite widely circulated and copied, the earliest extant text dating to the sixth century AD.

Strabo's *Geography* is a rather rambling work compiled largely from the works of others but with little apparent attempt to use the most up-to-date information. While its scope is admirably wide the work is geographically ill-balanced, being, understandably, biased towards the region the author knew well. He was not really interested in science, seeing little point in science for science's sake, and was particularly careless when attempting to handle these matters. All these shortcomings aside, as one recent commentator remarked, damning with faint praise, 'we owe him a vast debt for having survived . . .' In doing so his works preserved a huge body of data which would otherwise have been totally lost.

Strabo had a distinct view of geography – it was to be an adjunct to history, a background for the cultivated reader and a necessary source of information for the military and for Roman adminis-trators. A good recent parallel would be the Naval Intelligence Handbooks, written by a cabal of academic geographers during the Second World War, essentially as briefing documents on countries likely to be encountered by allied troops (and still, incidentally, a fascinating source, much sought after by book collectors). For Strabo, then, only the 'inhabited world' was relevant: it was useless to waste time in describing or speculating on remote areas: 'It is not necessary for those concerned with geography to bother about places outside of our own inhabited world, nor should the many and various differences in its measurements themselves be set out for a politician, like proofs they are hard dry things indeed' (2.5.34).

Strabo's first-hand knowledge of the west was severely limited, not least because he had travelled no further west than Italy, and on the more distant regions of the Atlantic he was more than usually muddled, although he seems to have created for himself a firmly held cognitive geography. The essential elements of this were that the Pyrenees and the Rhine ran north–south. West of the Pyrenees the north coast of Iberia lay east–west, while between the Pyrenees and the Rhine the coast of Keltikē ran reasonably straight from south-west to north-east. Britain, he believed, was about equal in length to Keltikē and lay closely alongside it, roughly parallel, with its north-eastern extremity, Kent, opposite the mouth of the Rhine. Ireland lay wholly north of Britain. It was 'an island not only remote beyond Britain but just barely habitable because of the cold'. He goes on to say that 'parts even more remote are considered uninhabitable'. Another of his misconceptions was that along any particular latitude the climate remained the same. This did not allow, for example, for the ameliorating effects of the Gulf Stream on the Atlantic coasts of Europe. For him the inhabitable world ended somewhere between 55 and 58°N: what are now Scotland and Denmark lay at the very margin.

How Strabo came to construct this curiously contorted geography is difficult to understand. During his childhood the Roman armies under Julius Caesar had rampaged across the whole of Gaul and knew well the maritime regions, and on two occasions Caesar had campaigned in Britain. In the aftermath, and throughout the time that Strabo was writing, the geography of Gaul became increasingly well known as the Roman administrative system took a hold, while, through regular trading expeditions, a more accurate knowledge of Britain would also have spread. With all this new information to hand it is surprising that Strabo stuck to his inaccurate and antiquated preconceptions. Yet he did so, defending them vehemently against any views that conflicted with his own.

The greatest source of conflict was the observations of Pytheas. It is not entirely clear whether Strabo had access to *On the Ocean*. There is certainly nothing in his writing to suggest that he was quoting directly from it and indeed on most occasions he makes clear that he is taking his information second-hand from other writers, such as Polybius, Timaeus, Eratosthenes, Dicaearchus and two we have not yet mentioned, Artemidorus and Posidonius. In any event what he learned of Pytheas' views he did not like at all.

The relationship of Spain, Keltikē and Britain did not fit his preconceptions – he could not accept the notion of the great westerly projection of Armorica nor the sailing times between Armorica and Britain, and as to the fact that Pytheas wrote of people living well beyond 55–58°N – this to him was sheer nonsense. His account of Thule was worthless since it dealt with the uninhabited region, and anyway 'anyone who made such continually false statements about well known places would scarcely be able to tell the truth about places which were not well known to everyone'. In other words Strabo is saying that since some of Pytheas' observations conflicted with Strabo's misconceived geography we must reject everything he says.

Strabo is therefore more than content to support Polybius in his damning rejection of Pytheas, adding his own particular invective. Pytheas was 'clearly shown to be the worst possible liar', he 'misled people who trusted him through ignorance', he 'had the audacity to falsify such matters', these things were 'all fabrications of Pytheas'. Only once is there a grudging acceptance that some of Pytheas' scientific observations may have been of use when Strabo admits, after referring to the remote north, 'one may, however, suppose he made use of the facts in observations of celestial phenomena and mathematical theory'. But then, by his own admission, matters of this kind were of little interest to him.

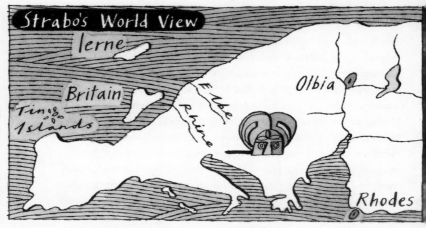

Strabo's World View

Ierne

Britain

Tin Islands

Elbe

Rhine

Olbia

Rhodes

The probability that Strabo relied entirely on secondary sources in referring to the views of Pytheas raises the question of whether or not *On the Ocean* was available to him, either when he visited Alexandria or indeed in any other library. Had it been available one might have expected him to have consulted it. Could it be that the book, along with many other priceless works, had been destroyed in the fire which swept the Great Library in March of 47 BC during Julius Caesar's siege of the Palace where his enemy Pompey was installed? It is entirely possible but, then, there were surely copies in other libraries. Hipparchus, the astronomer who worked for most of his life in Rhodes in the mid-second century BC, evidently had ready access to a text. Indeed, this could well have been the same copy that Geminus of Rhodes used when he was writing his own textbook on astronomy. Geminus quotes quite a long passage, in which Pytheas describes the shortness of the night in the extreme northern latitudes, directly from *On the Ocean*. Exactly when he composed his book is uncertain. Some scholars argue that it was as early as 30 BC but others would prefer to make it as late as AD 50: at any event it was well after the fire at the Great Library of Alexandria.

Three other writers of the first century AD make use of Pytheas. Two of them, Aëtius and Cleomedes, offer only passing reference but the third, Pliny the Elder, who died during the eruption of Vesuvius in AD 79, used the observations of Pytheas quite extensively in three of the thirty-seven books that comprise his *Natural History*. Pliny had the helpful practice of quoting his sources at the opening of each book. In Books 2, 4 and 37 Pytheas is specifically cited. He was evidently the authority for Pliny's description of Thule and Britain and his information about tin production in Cornwall and the Amber Coast and its islands, but how much of his information Pliny took directly from *On the Ocean* and how much he gathered from such secondary sources as Timaeus is uncertain. It is entirely possible that everything originating from Pytheas was quoted second-hand. If so then Geminus of Rhodes may well have been the last of our extant sources actually to have used *On the Ocean*.

Pliny did not know of Strabo's *Geography*, and although he had access to Polybius he was content to accept Pytheas as an entirely reliable observer.

Thereafter the trail goes cold. The mood of the world had changed and other subjects of more pressing interest occupy the writers of the next three centuries. Byzantine scholars of the fifth and sixth centuries make occasional reference to Pytheas and his observations but nine hundred years after his voyage their concern is largely antiquarian.

In recent times there has been much interest in Pytheas and his achievements and modern scholars are unanimous in their acceptance of his truthfulness and accuracy. M. Cary and E. H. Warmington, in their classic book *The Ancient Explorers*, published in 1929, allow themselves to reflect that 'In scientific discovery his journey was more fruitful than any preceding the age of Henry of Portugal' (i.e. the early fifteenth century AD). The circumpolar explorer Vilhjalmur Stefansson, whose book *Ultima Thule* was published in 1942, was more fulsome in his praise, concluding: 'He has been referred to as a Columbus with a flavour of Darwin; he seems to have been more nearly a composite of James Cook and Galileo.' So in spite of the vicious jealousy of Polybius and the muddled narrow-mindedness of Strabo, and their attempt to damn his

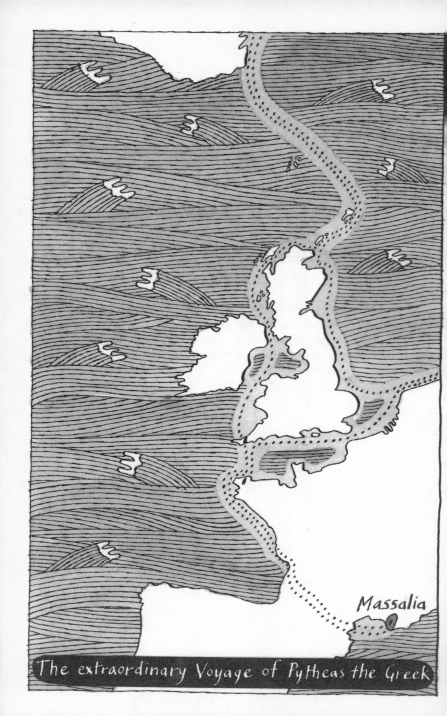

Massalia

The extraordinary Voyage of Pytheas the Greek

memory, the world has come to recognize the brilliant audacity of this shadowy Massaliot.

What manner of man he was we shall never know, but who could have made that journey without tenacity, fearlessness and an insatiable curiosity? And how did he spend the rest of his life after writing *On the Ocean*? On another expedition, perhaps one from which he never returned? Or did he while away his declining years in the waterfront bars of Massalia telling his stories to anyone prepared to listen? From here our imaginations, unrestrained by scraps of history and archaeology, can take full rein.

Postscript

Since publication of the hardback of *Pytheas* I have come across a curious story told by Diodorus Siculus of a mysterious island in the far north which, as we shall see, has some claim to be Lewis. Since Diodorus was quoting from the lost history of Hecataeus of Abdera, who was presumably using earlier sources, it is likely that errors and misunderstandings have crept in, but the essential points are clear

in the region beyond the land of the Celts [presumably here meaning Gaul] there lies in the ocean an island no smaller than Sicily. This island . . . is situated in the north and is inhabited by the Hyperboreans who are called by that name because their home is beyond the point where the north wind [Boreus] blows.   (Diodorus II, 47)

He goes on to say that Apollo was worshipped there (a reference most probably to a moon cult) in 'a notable temple which is adorned with many votive offerings and is spherical in shape'. The people of the island were 'most friendly disposed towards the Greeks' and the myth from which Diodorus quotes 'also relates that certain Greeks visited the Hyperboreans and left behind them costly votive offerings bearing inscriptions in Greek letters'.

So far there is nothing in the story to locate this northern island but then Diodorus provides the vital clues:

They say also that the moon, as viewed from this island, appears to be but a little distance above the earth . . . The account is also given that the god visits the island every nineteen years, the period in which the return of the stars to the same place in the heavens is accomplished; . . . At the time of this appearance of the god he both plays on the cithora [lyre] and dances continuously the night through from the vernal equinox until the rising of the Pleiades . . .   (Diodorus II, 47)

These lunar observations particularly intrigued the archaeo-astronomer Aubrey Burl when he came to write his book on mega-lithic stone circles and alignments, *From Carnac to Callanish* (1993). The nineteen-year interval between the major ceremonies of the Hyperboreans, to which Diodorus refers, is evidently the 18.61-year cycle governing the movement of the moon in these northern regions. But further precision is provided by the observa-tion of the moon skimming the horizon because it will appear to do this in the northern hemisphere only at or about the latitude 58° – the latitude of Lewis and the one upon which Pytheas made one of his sun-height measurements. Could then, Burl asked, the famous spherical temple of the Hyperboreans be the circle of standing stones on the hilltop of Callanish erected around 2800 BC? Here Diodorus' third observation is of particular help – the moon 'dances continuously the night through from the vernal equinox until the rising of the Pleiades'. If this is read to mean that at the spring equinox the moon was visible until the Pleiades (the Seven Sisters) rose in the sky this would be nonsense because at the spring equinox the Pleiades were in conjunction with the sun and therefore at sunrise would have been invisible in the sun's glare. A more sensible reading, as Burl has argued, is that the moon was seen to skim through the night sky from the time of the spring equinox (21 March) to the time that the Pleiades first became visible in the east at their dawn rising, an event which coincided with the Celtic ceremony of Beltane (1 May).

There is one final point to be made. From the great stone circle of Callanish alignments of standing stones run outwards roughly to the cardinal points. Detailed measurements have shown that one was directed towards the southern moonset, one to the equinoctial sunset and another to the dawn rising of the Pleiades.

All coincidence perhaps? Or compelling circumstantial evidence that the story of the Hyperboreans and their lunar temple derived from Pytheas and the conversations he had had with the people of Lewis proud to share folk traditions of their distant past with an inquisitive stranger as he trudged through the enveloping peat to see the famous old stones for himself.

Some Further Reading

I have deliberately kept the text of this book free of footnotes and references because they are so distracting to the reader who simply wants to follow the story. But for those who may want to follow up points raised here this brief endnote is added.

To enter the world of the Greek explorers it is difficult to better the exciting and authoritative book by Rhys Carpenter, *Beyond the Pillars of Hercules: The Classical World Seen Through the Eyes of its Discoverers* (1966: Delacorte Press, New York). There is a chapter devoted to Pytheas and his achievement is put into the broad perspective of Greek and Phoenician exploration. An earlier, and rather more academic, work on the same theme by M. Cary and E. H. Warmington, *The Ancient Explorers* (1929: Methuen, London), is also to be strongly recommended. Those with an appetite for an even more academic work, copiously referenced, might try J. O. Thomson's *History of Ancient Geography* (1948: Cambridge University Press). The name of Thule is discussed by G. Hattersley-Smith in *Mariner's Mirror* 72 (1986), 42.

There is of course a huge literature on the Greek world, which it would be invidious to try to signpost, but four works are of direct relevance to our theme. A. T. Hodge, *Ancient Greek France* (1998: Duckworth, London), provides a useful summary of Massalia (Marseille). Also highly recommended is an attractively illustrated and very up-to-date summary of the archaeology of Massalia and its hinterland by A. Hermary, A. Hesnard and H. Tréziny, *Marseille Grecque: La cité phocéenne (600–49 av. J.-C.)* (1999: Errance, Paris). A reader wishing to get to grips with the complexities of Greek astronomy, and who is not too frightened of a little mathematics, will find D. R. Dicks, *Early Greek Astronomy to Aristotle* (1970: Thames and Hudson, London), to be a very helpful introduction. For the more determined researcher, interested in the establishment of parallels of latitude, the same author's *The Geographical Fragments of Hipparchus* (1960: Athlone Press, London) is the source to use. The astronomy bound up in the megalithic stone circles and alignments of the Atlantic facade is brought together by Aubrey Burl in *From Carnac to Callanish* (1993: Yale University Press, New Haven).

Moving from the Mediterranean to the barbarian north, an outline of European Iron Age society at the time will be found in the present author's *The Ancient Celts* (1997: Oxford University Press). For more specific regional studies, Iron Age Armorica is thoroughly covered in P.-R. Giot, J. Briard and L. Pape, *Protohistoire de la Bretagne* (second edition 1995: Éditions Ouest-France, Rennes). For Britain, my *Iron Age Britain* (1995: Batsford/English Heritage, London) offers a short introduction, while *Iron Age Communities of Britain* (third edition 1991: Routledge, London) provides considerably more detail.

The ever-fascinating subject of ships and sailing is best approached through S. McGrail, *Ancient Boats in North-West Europe: The Archaeology of Water Transport to AD 1500* (second edition 1998: Longman, London).

Textual criticism of the classical writers is a vast and highly erudite field of study. Three works of direct relevance to our theme are F. W. Walbank, *Polybius* (1972: University of California Press, Berkeley), J. P. Murphy, *Rufus Festus Avienus, Ora Maritima* (1977: Ares Publishers, Chicago) and C. H. Roseman, *Pytheas of Massalia, On the Ocean* (1994: Ares Publishers, Chicago). This last volume is invaluable since it brings together all the texts which contain or refer to Pytheas' account of his journey (in the original Latin or Greek) and offers a critical commentary on them. It was Roseman who first suggested that Pytheas used local vessels – an idea which I have developed with enthusiasm.

Finally, for the real Pytheas enthusiast I offer a reasonably comprehensive list of the literature generated by the exploits of this ever-fascinating Greek.

1893   C. R. Markham, 'Pytheas the Discoverer of Britain', *Geographical Journal*, June 1893.

1893   G. Hergt, *Pytheas* (Halle).

1911   F. Nansen, *In Northern Mists* (London).

1929   M. Cary and E. H. Warmington, *The Ancient Explorers* (London), pp. 33–40.

1933   J. Malye, 'Pythéas', *Bulletin de l'Association Guillaume Budé*, October 1933 (Paris).

1936   G. E. Broche, *Pythéas le Massaliote* (Marseille).

1942   V. Stefansson, *Ultima Thule* (New York).

1952   H. J. Mette, *Pytheas von Massalia* (Berlin).

1954   E. Davin, 'Pythéas le Massaliote', *Bulletin de l'Association Guillaume Budé*, 2: 60–71.

1959   D. Stichtenoth, *Pytheas von Marseille, Über das Weltmeer* (Weimar–Cologne).

1966   R. Carpenter, *Beyond the Pillars of Hercules* (New York) (ch. V).

1975   P. Fabre, 'Étude sur Pythéas la Massaliote et l'Époque de ses Travaux', *Les Etudes Classiques*, 43: 25–44.

1975   C. F. C. Hawkes, *Pytheas: Europe and the Greek Explorers* (Oxford).

1981   I. Whitaker, 'The Problem of Pytheas' Thule', *Classical Journal*, 77: 148–64.

1985   R. Wenskus, 'Pytheas und der Bernsteinhandle', in K. Düwel et al., *Untersuchungen zu Handel und Verkehr der vor- und frügeschichtlichen Zeit in Mittel- und Nordeuropa*, i (Göttingen), pp. 84–108.

1994   C. H. Roseman, *Pytheas of Massalia: On the Ocean. Text, Translation and Commentary* (Chicago).

This present book is offered as a contribution to the continuing debate on Pytheas and in the hope that it will bring the achievements of this enigmatic character to the public he deserves.

A Note on the Translations Used

For the translations from the Greek and Roman writers I have used no particular authority, rather relying on several to produce the versions here given. Among the translations consulted are the various Loeb texts and those by P. Wiseman, J. J. Tierney, G. Rawlinson and C. H. Roseman. For the translation of Avienus, *Ora Maritima*, I have relied solely on that of J. P. Murphy given in his *Rufus Festus Avienus, Ora Maritima* (1977: Ares Publishers, Chicago).

Index

PENGUIN ONLINE

News, reviews and previews of forthcoming books

read about your favourite authors

•

investigate over 12,000 titles

•

browse our online magazine

•

enter one of our literary quizzes

•

win some fantastic prizes in our competitions

•

e-mail us with your comments and book reviews

•

instantly order any Penguin book

'To be recommended without reservation ... a rich and rewarding online experience' *Internet Magazine*

www.penguin.com

READ MORE IN PENGUIN

In every corner of the world, on every subject under the sun, Penguin represents quality and variety – the very best in publishing today.

For complete information about books available from Penguin – including Puffins, Penguin Classics and Arkana – and how to order them, write to us at the appropriate address below. Please note that for copyright reasons the selection of books varies from country to country.

In the United Kingdom: Please write to *Dept. EP, Penguin Books Ltd, Bath Road, Harmondsworth, West Drayton, Middlesex UB7 0DA*

In the United States: Please write to *Consumer Services, Penguin Putnam Inc., 405 Murray Hill Parkway, East Rutherford, New Jersey 07073-2136.* VISA and MasterCard holders call 1-800-631-8571 to order Penguin titles

In Canada: Please write to *Penguin Books Canada Ltd, 10 Alcorn Avenue, Suite 300, Toronto, Ontario M4V 3B2*

In Australia: Please write to *Penguin Books Australia Ltd, 487 Maroondah Highway, Ringwood, Victoria 3134*

In New Zealand: Please write to *Penguin Books (NZ) Ltd, Private Bag 102902, North Shore Mail Centre, Auckland 10*

In India: Please write to *Penguin Books India Pvt Ltd, 11 Community Centre, Panchsheel Park, New Delhi 110017*

In the Netherlands: Please write to *Penguin Books Netherlands bv, Postbus 3507, NL-1001 AH Amsterdam*

In Germany: Please write to *Penguin Books Deutschland GmbH, Metzlerstrasse 26, 60594 Frankfurt am Main*

In Spain: Please write to *Penguin Books S. A., Bravo Murillo 19, 1°B, 28015 Madrid*

In Italy: Please write to *Penguin Italia s.r.l., Via Vittorio Emanuele 45/a, 20094 Corsico, Milano*

In France: Please write to *Penguin France, 12, Rue Prosper Ferradou, 31700 Blagnac*

In Japan: Please write to *Penguin Books Japan Ltd, Iidabashi KM-Bldg, 2-23-9 Koraku, Bunkyo-Ku, Tokyo 112-0004*

In South Africa: Please write to *Penguin Books South Africa (Pty) Ltd, P.O. Box 751093, Gardenview, 2047 Johannesburg*